MIDDLE-CLASS MILLIONAIRE WOMEN

ESSENTIAL STRATEGIES TO ENSURE FINANCIAL LONGEVITY

CLARK A. KENDALL
CFA, AEP®, CFP®
FOUNDER AND CEO OF KENDALL CAPITAL

WITH CAROL L. PETROV, CFP®

www.mascotbooks.com

Middle-Class Millionaire Women:
Essential Strategies to Ensure Financial Longevity

For more information, please contact:
Mascot Books
620 Herndon Parkway, Suite 320
Herndon, VA 20170
info@mascotbooks.com

Library of Congress Control Number: 2020921857

CPSIA Code: PRFRE1220A

ISBN: 978-1-64543-781-9

Printed in Canada

To all of my women clients, past and present, who let me walk alongside them to help them meet their financial dreams.

Thank you for giving me the opportunity to serve you and your unique financial needs. I can only hope you have enjoyed the journey as much as I have. Unlike managing institutional money, helping individuals and families manage their money can make a more tangible, personal impact. It gives me particular satisfaction and confidence knowing that proper wealth management decisions do make a significant difference.

CONTENTS

INTRODUCTION

According to a recent study, there were 11.8 million U.S. millionaire households in 2018. Being a millionaire used to mean you were really wealthy. These days, $1 million is still a considerable amount of wealth, but depending on your cost of living and how long you'll live in retirement, you might need more than $1 million saved up by the time you leave work.

In *Middle-Class Millionaire*, I laid out the importance of accumulating $1 million+ in investable assets. I also described how middle-class people—everyday, hardworking people—could achieve lifelong financial security.

In this sequel, *Middle-Class Millionaire Women*, we look at everyday, hardworking women millionaires: Who are they? How do they create financial success? And why is it vitally important *for women especially* to take charge of their finances and ensure they achieve financial security?

The picture is sobering:

- On average, women outlive men by five years.

- Overall, women earn 80 cents to the dollar that men earn.

- Women take more time off work—for maternity leave, for longer periods of child rearing, to be caregivers for family members, and so on. Those interruptions can put a major dent in how much they earn, save, and contribute to Social Security during their careers.

- On top of that, many women are less confident about investing and tend to invest more conservatively. More-conservative investments tend to produce lower returns, and over the course of a lifetime, giving up a few percentage points in annual return can result in a gigantic gap in your accumulated assets.

Look at this hypothetical example:

$10,000 A YEAR INVESTED AT A	...4% ANNUAL RETURN	...6% ANNUAL RETURN	...8% ANNUAL RETURN
OVER 40 YEARS WILL GROW TO...	$764,000+	$1.09 million	$1.584 million

Have I depressed you? That's not my intention. The message is clear: overall—*and please understand the importance of generalizing here!*—women need to save more, invest more aggressively, and take charge of their financial lives to ensure their future financial well-being.

While this is true for single women, it is also true for married women. Divorced and widowed women can sometimes have a rude awakening when their world suddenly changes and they need to do more with less, and with less guidance.

These rude awakenings can happen on an individual, personal level or more globally, as many of us experienced recently with the financial challenges presented by the coronavirus pandemic and its economic impact.

As with *Middle-Class Millionaire*, in this book I weave in the stories of clients whose situations readers might relate to (the names have been changed, so no worries regarding confidentiality or privacy!). We all can learn—from our own experiences, and from those of others—with the goal of greater personal financial success. Sometimes those experiences are lessons to be learned regarding mistakes to be avoided. And sometimes they are successes we can be inspired by.

This book is structured so as to share broadly relevant information along with advice that can help women in specific situations. The book has five sections. The first part, including this introduction, provides an overview of the need for greater financial literacy, confidence, and involvement of women in their personal finances. It also takes a high-level look at how women differ from men as investors.

Part 2 addresses a variety of common concerns and provides a woman's outlook on some critical financial topics. The chapters focus on managing the most important risks; how to maintain your perspective (and your sanity!) when financial markets become unsettled and unsettling; how best to look for and get financial advice; how to live within your means, which is the key to becoming a middle-class millionaire; how to make sure your money lasts as long as you will; and how to juggle competing priorities.

Part 3 focuses on specific situations women often encounter. These include sudden changes to financial life caused by divorce or widowhood; issues relating to single women; the need for caregivers to not neglect themselves financially and otherwise; and the risks faced by married women who are not fully involved in family finances.

We take a step back in part 4 and examine women and money through the lens of life stages. We begin with best practices on how to raise financially savvy children; how to establish a strong financial base as a young woman; how to catch up on saving and investing or turbocharge them in midlife if you have to; and finally, tips on how to go the distance financially, addressing concerns that women tend to face later in life.

We wrap it all up in the final section with a summary of the book's key points and action steps you can apply to your own life so that you can thrive as a middle-class millionaire woman!

Are you a middle-class millionaire woman? Would you like to become one, or help teach your daughters to achieve financial responsibility and security? Please read on.

CLARK A. KENDALL
CFA, AEP®, CFP®
FOUNDER AND CEO OF KENDALL CAPITAL
ROCKVILLE, MARYLAND

SECTION I

Venus, Mars, and Your Money

CHAPTER 1
This Book Is for *You*

S hould you read this book? Are you a woman who would like to know more about how anyone can become financially secure? Would you like to read about how others have done this through simple, commonsense strategies? Would you simply like to become more conversant in personal financial matters and less dependent on others?

Do you know a woman—possibly your wife, sister, or daughter—who could benefit from knowing more about personal finance and investments and how to avoid costly mistakes? This book could be for them.

The following are just a few scenarios this book covers about how to grow your wealth slowly and steadily (no get-rich-quick promises), how to overcome the financial obstacles many women face, and how to make sure you don't outlive your money.

HAPPILY NEVER AFTER?

Jane *is a stay-at-home mom. As a result, she has not earned a salary, made contributions to Social Security, or saved for her retirement.*

She figures that's fine, because her husband, a doctor with a secure, well-paying job, will take care of her as he always has. But then one day, Jane learns that her dreams of happily-ever-after won't materialize, because divorce looms large. How can she learn all she needs to know in order to survive financially?

TILL DEATH DO YOU PART…AND THEN?

Peggy has worked her whole life as part of a dual-income couple, and she's been disciplined, managing to save a decent portion of what she has earned. She knows the basics of personal financial management, but she has left a lot of the details to her partner. That was fine until her spouse died. Now a grieving widow in her 60s, Peggy needs to carry on without her loved one by her side making those big decisions. What can or should Peggy do now? How does she know what to do or whom to lean on?

A MIDLIFE FINANCIAL CRISIS?

Karen is good at saving money, but she has never felt comfortable with investing risks. The very word "risk" scares her. She is terrified of losing money. As a result, she has squirreled away almost all her savings in ultra-"safe" low-risk, low-yielding products. But after a recent financial checkup, Karen—now in her mid-40s—is beginning to rethink this approach as she wonders whether she'll ever have enough saved to afford to retire. Maybe it's time for a financial makeover.

These are three scenarios depicting vulnerability. This isn't to say all or even most women are financially vulnerable, dependent, or lacking in confidence or knowledge. I present these scenarios here to show you the risks that exist when we rely too heavily on others or don't invest the time or make the effort to be more financially aware and capable.

Middle-Class Millionaire Women takes you through various scenarios and anecdotes, situations, statistics, and common financial challenges women face as they go through life. Ready to learn more?

In the next brief chapter, we explore some of the tendencies women often bring to how they manage their personal finances and investments, and how these traits can be advantageous when applied thoughtfully. Again, any generalities are not intended as universal truths. Instead, they reflect common tendencies that I have observed in my three decades of serving middle-class millionaires.

CHAPTER 2
Advantage: Women

Women vary greatly in their approach to investing, but they tend to share some common characteristics, some of which put them at an advantage over men.

Overall, women tend to be more cautious or conservative with investing than men. While that can be to their detriment if taken to an extreme, when women use that caution as a restraint on ego and excessive risk-taking, it can also be a major advantage.

HUMILITY IS A POSITIVE TRAIT

One classic mistake that many investors make is to think they're smarter or better investors than they are. It's easy to fall into that trap. A good experience with an investment may lead you to interpret that success as a sign that you are smarter than the market. That false confidence could lead you to take excessive or ill-advised risks, which could set you up for a fall.

A more cautious and humble approach would be to question whether luck played a role in your success. Of course, it could be skill *and* luck! The key is that by remaining humble, you might maintain more of a skeptical and objective outlook, and that could help you manage risks more effectively. In our experience, many women investors tend to be humbler than men. And that is in their best interest.

Maggie is a 70-year-old divorced woman with no children or family members. Her $1.7 million of investments is split roughly between an individual retirement account (IRA) and a taxable account. For monthly income, she receives about $3,000 in Social Security and pension benefits. To live comfortably, she needs another $3,000–$4,000 per month.

Her problem, when she came to us, was that more than 30 percent of her assets were invested in one stock, evenly divided between her taxable account and her IRA. The stock had been a favorite of her father's, so she bought a lot of it and opted for the dividends to be reinvested in more shares. The issue is that with such a heavy concentration in this one security, it would end up dictating what she would and wouldn't be able to do for the rest of her life.

Before hiring us to manage her funds, Maggie would closely read the stock's quarterly earnings report and do research on the company's products and services. But she lacked the skills to do proper research, and she knew it. So she was receptive to us rebalancing and de-risking her portfolio. We did that by using short-term, more-conservative investment products for her short-term needs and a well-diversified set of securities to be held for the long term, which were designated to meet her long-term needs. She was relieved that she was no longer dependent on a single company's stock price, and she was no longer worried about whether she understood the implications of the company's financial reports.

LESS (ACTIVITY) CAN BE MORE
(MONEY IN YOUR ACCOUNT)

Women tend to be less interested in the "sport" or "challenge" of investing and trying to outperform the market. Instead, they generally are more interested in long-term, bottom-line results. And that, as we'll see in an anecdote and a famous study, can be an advantage. Being less absorbed in investing minutiae and less inclined to trade (too) frequently can be to your benefit. As the counterintuitive saying goes, less is more, at least in certain things.

In general, investors can be their own worst enemy. As humans, we tend to make mistakes. Hey, we're only human! We tend to react and overreact to short-term market movements. And if we're investing for the long term, then short-term market movements have little bearing on our success in reaching long-term goals.

We often do the exact opposite of what a given situation calls for. We buy high—when the market has already soared—and sell low—after the market has crashed. That's because of our emotions and lack of discipline in sticking with an investment plan—if we even have an investment plan.

CHUCK AND BETH, A MODERN FABLE

This is where women tend to have the upper hand on men. I have a doozy of a story involving a couple of friends, Chuck and Beth. You could fairly say that Chuck was full of himself.

He loved to think he was smarter than the financial markets. A little early success might have gone to his head.

In 2014, after Facebook stock had doubled in the two years following its initial public offering, Chuck was sure it was set for a crash or at least a major correction. Its price-to-earnings valuation was sky high, and he recalled what had happened to dot-com stocks. So he decided to short Facebook stock. That means basically betting that the stock will go down. Instead of making money if the stock rises in value, you lose if it rises and win if it falls.

There are a couple of big problems with shorting stock. First, we're not able to predict the future as much as we'd like to think we are. Second, if a stock that you have shorted rises and keeps rising, there's no limit to how much you could lose. That's if you don't use something called a put option, which, for a price, gives you the option to buy a stock that has fallen without committing your money up front and risking that it will rise.

I won't bore you with more details. Simply, Chuck went all in with no safeguard. He was fully exposed to risk. Wait, it gets worse. Chuck did something very aggressive. He leveraged his short. Leveraging means multiplying your risk. He doubled the amount he could gain if the stock fell or lose if it rose. You could say he was greedy. You could also say he was foolish, and not in the Motley Fool sense!

Pardon the pun, but I bet you can tell where this story is going. Facebook stock didn't drop. It rose higher and higher. It has more than tripled in value since January 2014, when Chuck double-shorted it. He eventually reluctantly washed his hands of this investment mistake, losing every dollar he had gambled with.

Now for Beth, Chuck's friend. Next to him, anyone would look brilliant. Beth simply listened to our advice when she asked about Chuck's strategy or wild gamble. We advised her against taking such risks. She listened to us, and her diversified portfolio has gained substantially, reflecting the overall gain in financial markets since early 2014.

After that wild story, it might be overkill or anticlimactic to cite an academic study, but it very much validates the anecdotal evidence depicted in Chuck's behavior. A few years ago, a famous study called "Why Do Investors Trade Too Much?" looked at the drawbacks of trading too often. In the study, two professors at University of California–Berkley, Brad Barber and Terrence Odean, found that the more people traded, the less they earned on their investments. The 20 percent of investors who traded the most earned 7.2 percentage points per year less in returns than the least-active investors. And they found that men tend to be more overconfident than women and traded 45 percent more actively than women.[1]

So Beth's friend Chuck was just a more pronounced example of a well-established tendency.

In summary, I believe that women tend to manage money from the heart. They're more goals based and less competitive than men. They invest for a reason, and they retain that perspective. They have a clearer picture of where they want to go. If I can toss in an analogy from the world of sports, men play baseball to hit the ball out of the park, while women play baseball to win the game. And that means they strike out a lot less!

---

[1]   http://www.triplepartners.com/wp-content/uploads/Why-do-Investors-trade-too-much_Barber-Odean-2006.pdf

OPEN TO RECEIVING PROFESSIONAL HELP

Another advantage to being less preoccupied with beating the market and to having less ego invested is that women tend to be more open and receptive to receiving investment advice. As we will explore more deeply in Chapter 5, getting professional advice from an experienced, qualified "fiduciary" advisor—that means someone who is on your side, with no vested interest or conflict of interest—can be invaluable.

Broadly speaking, do-it-yourselfers can sometimes do a good job. However, hiring a pro often pays off in the long run, and that can apply to a home renovation, auto repair, or achieving optimal results with your investment portfolio. When interviewing a professional advisor, be sure to ask how they are compensated and whether they receive any benefit from recommending some investments over others. You should be able to understand easily how much of your performance may be offset by fees—whether those fees are hidden or transparent.

So, if you think that you might be at a disadvantage as an investor and as a consumer of financial services because you're less knowledgeable or less interested than some men you know, you can now see that isn't necessarily a drawback.

In summary, it is likely to your advantage as an investor if you:

- Are humble and recognize your limits.

- Don't try to outdo or outthink the financial markets.

- Don't trade stocks or other securities too often, leaving yourself vulnerable to ill-considered moves and racking up needless trading expenses.

- Make thoughtful decisions.

- Don't confuse investing with gambling.

With that being said, however, even when relying on or working with a professional, it is important for you to know and understand the basics of personal finance and investing. Financial literacy is a significant and highly costly problem in our society. So keep reading further to learn more as a *Middle-Class Millionaire Woman.*

SECTION II

Common Concerns

CHAPTER 3
Risk Matters

O ne of the most important aspects of personal finance—and one of the most misunderstood—is risk. Yes, risk is a four-letter word. It can be your nemesis and thwart your efforts to reach your financial goals. But it can be managed. However, before we can manage risk effectively, we need to understand it.

MORE THAN VOLATILITY

One common misconception about risk is that it's the same as volatility, or the short-term ups and downs of the financial markets. It's true that volatility is a form of risk, and the chance of losing money when your investments fall in value is real. But there's a lot more to risk than the rise and fall of the stock market.

WHAT IS RISK?

The general definition of risk is "exposure to danger, harm, or loss." As you know, it can be risky to drive a car too fast, under the influence of alcohol, or when you are tired or distracted. It's also risky to ride in a car without a seat belt. It's risky for children to play in the street or to take a ride from a stranger.

Financial risks are a bit less clear than those physical types of risk, but they can be just as devastating. What makes matters worse is that many people don't understand financial risks, or they think they do, but they're focused on the wrong types of risk. Here's a brief overview of a few key risks that you might face with your investments:

INFLATION RISK

A long-term risk we all face is that over time, our purchasing power will decrease. That can happen when the cost of living (the rate of inflation) rises at a faster pace than the return on our investments or savings. For example, if inflation is running at 3 percent annually and your investments earn 2 percent, you'll lose about 1 percent of purchasing power per year. Over a long period, like 20–30 years, that steady erosion of your purchasing power could be painful. It's like your money is shrinking rather than growing.

CONCENTRATION RISK

Concentration risk is the risk of having too much of your money invested in, or concentrated in, a single stock or group of stocks or in just one industry or economic sector. The concentration of your investment magnifies the impact of any gains or losses. What if something catastrophic happened to that one stock that you are concentrated in? Do you recall Enron in 2000–2001? The energy and commodities company's stock plummeted from $90 per share in August 2000 to $0.26 in December 2001. A friend of mine thought the falling stock was a bargain, so he bought more shares. In the investment world, that's known as trying to catch a falling knife or throwing good money after bad. Definitely not recommended!

Another friend graduated from the University of Maryland with a degree in electrical engineering and computer science in the mid-1980s and got a relatively high-paying job at General Electric after graduation. For the next 15 years, he received stock options and was able to buy GE stock at a discount to fair market value. Wisely, he took advantage of these programs, and by the turn of the century, he owned more than $500,000 of GE stock.

Because his other holdings were worth less than $50,000, he had an extremely concentrated stock portfolio of GE. In the year 2000, I recommended that he diversify his portfolio away from this one stock of a company that also employed him. He thought, "Why sell this great security? After all, GE is a diversified company." He also didn't want to pay the capital gains taxes, which would have been more than $100,000.

In retrospect, perhaps paying taxes on a gain wouldn't have been such a bad thing, because today, 20 years later, GE stock is worth one-eighth the value it was in 2000. Owning a concentrated portfolio of one or two stocks is not investing, it is gambling.

A more recent example is the performance of the volatile energy sector over the past few years. In 2015, the U.S. energy sector lost 21 percent. In 2016, it gained 28 percent. In 2017, it was relatively flat, with a 1 percent loss. In 2018, it lost another 18 percent. And in 2019, it gained 12 percent.[2] Compare that with the overall stock market, as reflected by the S&P 500 Index.[3] In four of the five years, the energy sector trailed the overall U.S. stock market by double digits.

	U.S. ENERGY SECTOR	S&P 500 INDEX	DIFFERENCE IN RETURNS—ENERGY STOCKS VERSUS OVERALL MARKET
2015	-21.47%	-0.73%	-20.74%
2016	27.95%	9.54%	+18.41%
2017	-1.01%	19.42%	-20.43%
2018	-18.10%	-6.24%	-11.86%
2019	11.87%	28.88%	-17.01%

You can see that if you had a heavy concentration in that one sector, it would have added substantially to the stock market's annual ups and downs, and you would have trailed it significantly.

Quite simply, investing is risky enough, but concentrating your investments in a single stock or sector will increase your exposure to risk, magnifying your gains or losses. In my

[2] https://finance.yahoo.com/quote/XLE/performance/

[3] https://www.macrotrends.net/2526/sp-500-historical-annual-returns

opinion, life is too short for wild gambles, and most people I know prefer to be able to sleep at night.

LIQUIDITY RISK

Being able to access your money quickly and easily is known as liquidity. The risk that you won't be able to access your investments when you want to withdraw money or sell shares is known as liquidity risk. Most stocks and bonds are highly liquid, meaning you can sell shares the day that you want to and receive money a few days later, once the trade is settled.

In sharp contrast, private equity investments are quite illiquid. Investors understand that they will have to lock up their money for a while, possibly several years. In return for that illiquidity, they hope for a higher rate of return, but that's far from a certainty.

LONGEVITY RISK

If you are investing in a retirement plan, the biggest risk you'll face isn't short-term market volatility. It's the risk that you could outlive your savings. This is particularly true for women, because they live longer than men on average. There are a number of ways to manage or minimize this risk. Here are three methods that I agree with and one that I am not a fan of:

1. Saving enough for your retirement.

2. Investing for long-term growth so that you take advantage of the opportunity to earn long-term higher compound growth. This generally means having a good portion allocated

to a diversified mix of so-called risk assets, including stocks, real estate, commodities, high-yield bonds, and other investments with relatively high growth potential and volatility. They might rise and fall in value but also reward investors with higher potential returns.

3. Monitoring your assets and your budget carefully year after year and adapting as needed.

4. Purchasing a guaranteed life annuity with some of your money so you are assured of at least a certain secure basic level of income for the rest of your life.

I am not a fan of annuities. Most of the guaranteed life annuities will pay the annuitant 5 percent per year. This means you need to live 20 years to have your money returned to you, and only in year 21 would you start to receive any return on your investment. Another big disadvantage of annuities is that if you are diagnosed with terminal cancer and given three years to live, you might want to ask the annuity company to pay your next three years of income, which would allow you to go on a round-the-world trip while you are still able to. But no annuity company will do anything more than pay you your monthly, quarterly, or annual income while you are alive.

We'll get into more detail on how to manage longevity risk in Chapter 7.

These risks—inflation, concentration, liquidity, and longevity—are just a few of the most relevant risks investors face. It's important to be as aware of them as you are of market volatility, the type of risk that we sometimes pay too much attention to.

THINK OF YOUR TIME LINE

One of the most important things to consider is your investment time line. For short-term investments, market volatility is typically the key risk to be aware of and to try to manage. For long-term investments, such as your retirement savings, you can ride out short-term market movements. But if you're invested too conservatively, in a so-called "safe" investment that won't go down in value but also won't rise much, that could actually be much riskier than a more volatile investment over the long term.

THE RULE OF 72

The problem is that the 2 percent annual income you might earn on a CD will take forever to grow. Let's use the Rule of 72, which says to divide the number 72 by your annual rate of return to see how long it will take to double your investment's value. 72 / 2 = 36. If you earn a steady 2 percent return, it would take 36 years to double your investment's value. That's three and a half decades.

Contrast that with a 10 percent average annual return on stocks—no guarantee you'll earn that, but over the past 100 years or so, that's been the average historical return. Divide 72 by 10 = roughly 7 years. So, in 35 years, a sum of $10,000 would double in 7 years, double again in 14 years, double a third time in 21 years, a fourth time in 28 years, and a fifth time in 35 years. This is all hypothetical and for illustrative purposes only, but $10,000 x 2 x 2 x 2 x 2 x 2 = $20,000…$40,000…$80,000

...$160,000...$320,000. Let's go back to that 2 percent return. In that case, your $10,000 would double once, to $20,000.

That's enough theory. Let's look at a couple of real examples to show what I'm talking about.

TOO CONSERVATIVE FOR TOO LONG

In 2018, Jane, a 69-year-old prospective client, walked into our office and said she wanted to retire next year. Jane was single and earned about $50,000 per year working for the federal government. She had contributed 3 percent of her salary each year to the federal Thrift Savings Plan (TSP) program. She had invested in the stock index fund up until she looked at her year-end statement in 2008.

When Jane saw that her account balance had declined by more than 30 percent from the previous year, she panicked. She immediately stopped contributing to her retirement account and moved her entire balance from the stock index fund to a short-term government securities fund. This locked in what would have been just a temporary loss, or loss "on paper" as we say in the industry.

For the next 10 years, from 2008 to 2018, Jane's retirement account balance grew at just a 1–2 percent annual rate in the safe but low-yielding conservative money market fund. After 10 years, it had still not recovered all of what it had lost in 2008.

Her retirement account balance was about $130,000, and even though Jane had delayed collecting Social Security benefits so that she could receive the maximum monthly benefit, she was only expecting about $2,300 a month in benefits.

That wouldn't be enough to live on along with a safe level of withdrawal from her modest $130,000 nest egg, which might have come to roughly $425 a month.

At age 69, Jane still had a mortgage on her home. She considered moving to Seattle to live near her son, but she discovered that Seattle was even more expensive than Washington, D.C. Sadly, she realized too late that investing too conservatively can be as risky or costly as being too aggressive with your investments. Because of her fears, she had also stopped contributing to her retirement account when she would have benefited greatly from dollar-cost averaging.

The unfortunate outcome for Jane is that she likely will have limited retirement options for the rest of her life. She did not become a client of Kendall Capital, but I suspect Jane will still have to work some type of job in her 70s in order to make ends meet.

DON'T LET ONE STOCK DICTATE
YOUR FINANCIAL FUTURE

Back in the early 1990s, one of my close childhood school friends became one of the first 100 employees of a new company called America Online, better known as AOL. She was awarded stock options that a decade later were worth more than $2 million. For her, that was like winning the lottery—$2 million from this one security!

In reality, her AOL stock options weren't really worth $2 million, because there would be a major tax drag on that money. Whenever she sold her AOL stock, she would have to pay roughly $500,000 in federal, state, and local capital gains taxes. Then AOL stock declined, and she resisted selling until she finally determined that as the stock's price fell, she had just enough to pay off her $500,000 mortgage.

She finally sold it all at 25 percent of the peak share price for AOL stock. I am the first to admit that it is virtually impossible to pick the very bottom to know when to buy a stock or the very top to know when it's best to sell. The classic mistake my elementary school friend made was to base her entire financial fortune on this one security. It's true that Jeff Bezos, Bill Gates, and Steve Jobs, the billionaire founders of Amazon, Microsoft, and Apple, respectively, all benefited enormously from the success of a single concentrated security. But for every Bezos, Gates, or Jobs, there are thousands of investors who fall far short and subject themselves to huge risks.

When you own a diversified portfolio of securities, you can become less emotional about any one security and gradually buy into undervalued securities and out of overpriced ones. By having a disciplined process in place as opposed to owning just one security, you'll be protected when—not if—you make a mistake with any one investment, and you won't risk your financial future on it.

RISK: THE TAKEAWAY

The lesson I would love for all readers and middle-class millionaire women clients of mine to learn and retain is that there are many risks related to personal finance and investing. To manage those risks well, it helps to keep them all in perspective and to neither fixate on any single risk, such as volatility, nor ignore any risk, such as having too concentrated an exposure to any one investment.

When it comes to retirement investing and the greatest risk of all, longevity risk, we always need to think of the big picture. Like marathoners, we need to pace ourselves and be able to go the distance. At times it can be tricky when we don't really know where the finish line will be. Imagine being a long-distance runner and not knowing where the race ends!

So be smart, be wise, don't expose yourself to too much risk, and always keep the big picture in mind. Speaking of which, turn the page to learn more about perspective in the next chapter, "It's the Forest, Not the Trees."

CHAPTER 4

It's the Forest, Not the Trees

Perhaps you've heard the expression "we're our own worst enemy" or "we're only human." These truisms often apply to the world of personal investing. Because we tend to be driven by emotional responses to things like market rallies and crashes, we often do the exact worst thing we possibly could.

For example, we buy stocks *after* the market rises, and we sell *after* the market tumbles. Now, if you know the basics of investing, you know "Buy high and sell low" is not the mantra of successful investors. To put it in a different framework, imagine rushing to the supermarket after the price of your favorite item rises 10 percent or 20 percent to stock up on it, rather than bargain shopping!

The effect of this type of reactive, emotional behavior and a slew of other mistakes investors tend to make is that although the S&P 500 Index averaged a return of 9.85 percent a year for the 20 years ending on December 31, 2015, the average equity investor earned just 5.19 percent, according to research by Dalbar Inc.[4] That's a gap of 4.66 percent on average.

---

[4] https://www.thebalance.com/why-average-investors-earn-below-average-market-returns-2388519

Looking at the performance gap more closely for 2018, the overall average investor's return for the year was a loss of 9.42 percent, while the S&P 500 Index lost just 4.38 percent. The average stock investor—whom we'll call Charlie—underperformed the broad stock benchmark by 5.04 percent in 2018. How did the investors do so poorly? A closer look reveals that Charlie sold some stocks but not enough to avoid losses. Then, compounding that, Charlie was out of the market to some degree when the stock market was recovering its losses, missing out on the rebound and its gains.

I'd say that's a perfect illustration of how market timing doesn't work. We don't have crystal balls. So at best we'll bet correctly half the time, not only locking in what would have otherwise been "paper" losses but possibly creating unnecessary tax events if we're trading outside of a retirement account. For example, we have a client, Sharon, who worked in the technology field through the booming '90s. Sharon was top in her field, and she invested in what she knew. However, when the tech bubble burst, dragging down good companies with bad, she watched the value of her investment account get cut in half. In 2001, she couldn't stand to watch her stocks continue to flounder, and she decided half was better than nothing. So she sold everything to buy herself a vacation home.

Today, 18 years later, she still carries $62,000 in realized losses as she slowly offsets them against new gains in her taxable account. While she loves her vacation home, the tax losses are an annual reminder that she made an emotional decision about her investments. As horrible as the bubble burst in 2000 was for most investors, had they stayed firm and held onto a diversified portfolio, they would have seen their account back where it had been by 2007, fully recouping their losses in seven years.

This was one of the most dramatic and prolonged drops in the stock market's history, and it still recovered in just seven years. That's why, as a general rule of thumb, it's good to consider "long-term" investments in the stock market to be for money you won't need for at least 7–10 years.

MEET SAM, MY CLIENT MARKET INDICATOR

I have something that I call my "client market indicator." It's not scientific or sophisticated, but anecdotally, it tells me something valuable. When I get two panicky client calls within one week, it tells me to buy index call options, because there's a good chance that the market is going to go up. It's a classic contrarian indicator.

One day in 2012, when the market had been particularly volatile, a client—we'll call him Sam—called and asked me to sell him out of everything. He said he couldn't handle it. I told him he was my client market indicator.

Sam was puzzled and surprised. "Really? What do you do?" I told him I buy index options, basically doing the opposite of a panicky client. He said, "Wow!" And he realized that maybe he should hold off on doing something rash. But a half hour later, Sam called me again and said, "I don't care. Just sell me out."

Predictably, the market rallied 5 percent the next week. Sam called me back after the rally and asked, "Did you make money?" I said I did, and I thanked him with a chuckle. And then guess what? Sam wanted to come back into the market!

To women's credit, this client market indicator overreaction is typically a male phenomenon. Very few women clients of Kendall Capital have this tendency. They tend to sit tight, not second-guess us, and follow our advice.

But women too can get nervous and do the wrong thing or be tempted to. So let's delve a little more deeply into the psychology of investing and what trips us up, and then learn how we can counter that so we can stop being our own worst enemies or at least minimize the damage we can do to our financial future.

A QUICK LESSON ON BEHAVIORAL FINANCE: SIX CLASSIC IRRATIONAL BIASES

The study of how and why we make ill-considered, emotion-driven investment decisions is called behavioral finance. Here are a half-dozen classic irrational biases that behavioral finance researchers have uncovered:

1. Overconfidence: Often we're not as smart or as good as we think we are as investors. That overconfidence can lead us to trade more often and to make more mistakes. The good news for women is that men are much more prone to this tendency. Recall the study by Brad Barber and Terrence Odean, mentioned in Chapter 2, in which men traded 45 percent more than women. The one-fifth of investors who traded the most trailed the least-active investors by 7.2 percentage points per year. Also, single men traded 67 percent more than single women. So women can do relatively well as investors just by being themselves. Not overconfident.

2. Loss aversion: Being averse to losing money, when taken to an extreme, can play out in a couple of negative ways. One is to be overly conservative and deny yourself the potential to earn a reasonable return with your overly safe investments. The other is that by overreacting to a short-term market loss, ignoring a longer-term or broader trend of gains, you might hit the "sell switch." By panic selling, you would lock in a loss when a cooler, calmer approach might allow the volatility to play out. Think of people like Jane, the 69-year-old woman in Chapter 3 who bailed from stocks in 2008 and missed a decade of great returns.

3. Fear of regret: We don't like to admit when we are wrong, because it hurts to admit mistakes. The way this sometimes plays out with investments is that we tend to hold onto losing investments too long, not wanting to face up to the mistake. And by doing that, we can compound the loss. Yes, we're human. Yes, we make mistakes. Recognize it. Own it. Or sell it! And move on.

4. Anchoring: Sometimes we get so caught up in recent events that we lose our perspective. That habit of overemphasizing the most recent performance or event can distort our thinking and lead us to irrational or ill-advised actions. That's known as anchoring. An example might be if the stock market fell 10 percent over the course of a couple of months. That might make us feel the recent loss more intensely and forget about any gains the stocks had made in previous years.

5. Selective listening/prejudging/mental accounting: There are a number of descriptions for this trait, which is to play mental games to justify anything—your own preconceived notions or biases or denial of the facts. Picture someone with their fingers in their ears, saying, "I can't hear you!" Seriously, when we can't be objective, we can get into deep trouble, especially where money is concerned.

6. Herding: This describes following the herd, whether it's buying dot-com stocks; real estate, which "can't possibly lose value" (until it does); Bitcoin; or whatever the latest thing is that everyone is talking about and buying. This is a recipe for failure, because it typically involves buying high and selling low.

So, now that we know about the dangers of overconfidence, loss aversion, fear of regret, anchoring, mental accounting, and herding, what can we do about it?

Plenty.

TEN WAYS YOU CAN PROTECT YOURSELF FROM YOUR OWN WORST TENDENCIES

1. Have a plan. If you fail to plan, you are planning to fail! A financial plan gives you structure and can keep you on track, protecting you from the volatility of your emotions.

2. Allocate appropriately. The cornerstone of your investment plan should be your asset allocation. It's good to review it, and if you see the need to change your allocation to stocks, bonds, and cash, and to subcategories, that's fine. But changes to your investments should be done within that disciplined framework, not based on your emotional mood on any given day.

3. Build a buffer. By having more-conservative investments for your short- and midterm needs, you give yourself breathing room and comfort knowing volatility won't hurt your ability to meet those goals. This simple rule allows for more aggressive investments to work for you in the longer-term segment or tranche. In fact, when you follow this rule *and* keep adding to your long-term investments, you'll benefit overall from investing during market dips, and you'll still sleep at night knowing your short- and midterm goals are covered. Remember Jane from the previous chapter? One of the big mistakes she made was that she didn't keep adding to the stock market after the 2008 crash.

4. Always remember the big picture. Don't get caught up in short-term-itis. Watch and read less, not more, of the financial media. Don't look at your portfolio balance every day or every week. Quarterly reviews are fine. Remember what you are saving or investing for, and recognize that the daily market noise is just that—noise. Tune it out.

5. Have realistic expectations. Understand that more-aggressive investments, such as stocks, do rise and fall in value, but over the longer term, they have tended to outperform less-volatile investments. One reason is that risk and reward go hand in hand. Investors are compensated for taking more risk by receiving higher potential returns. There are no guarantees.

And that is part of having realistic expectations. But Warren Buffett didn't become one of the wealthiest people in the world by buying Treasury securities.

6. Check less often. See #4: Always remember the big picture. Find other things to do with your time and your focus. Bake a cake for your friend's party instead of buying one. Try a new style of yoga. Call a friend you haven't seen in years. Watch a movie with your child or grandchild. Play pickleball with your partner. There's a gazillion fun things to do rather than calculate how much "unrealized" wealth you gained or lost today or last week. "Unrealized" means that until you actually sell an investment, you haven't "realized" the loss. Because it's just a loss on paper, it could reverse course. That's why we recommend you check on a quarterly basis, as it's better for your overall health and well-being to spend precious time on activities that enrich your life, while still staying aware and engaged with your investment strategies.

It's like weighing yourself too often when you're trying to lose weight. It's best to just stick with a disciplined long-term plan for exercise and healthy eating.

7. Do less. Trade less often. Buying and selling and thinking about what to buy and sell costs you. I referred to the tendency of frequent traders to do poorly relative to the overall market. One reason is that we make mistakes. The more we try to outsmart the market, the more opportunities we have to make mistakes. But also, every time you pull the trigger on a stock purchase or sale, you incur trading fees or commissions and possibly have tax consequences. As Gene Fama, Nobel laureate in economics, said, "Your money is like a bar of soap. The more you handle it, the less you have." Just do less.

8. Work with a pro. You hire a professional to fix your car or sell your house. You hire a pro to style your hair. You might have hired a professional wedding planner, event organizer, interior decorator…the list is long. Work with a disciplined, expert, fiduciary financial advisor who will put his or her experience and knowledge to work for you.

In the case of Kendall Capital, we have three Chartered Financial Analysts® (CFAs®) on staff, who are experts in managing portfolios. As CFAs®, they—and our clients—benefit from the knowledge, perspective, and discipline that come with a degree in financial analysis, and the rigorous standards inherent in earning the CFA® degree, acknowledged by Investopedia as "the gold standard in the field of investment analysis." Read more about the benefit of receiving unbiased professional financial advice in the next chapter, "Advice on Advice."

9. Stay the course. You have a plan. Great. Follow it. Let it and your financial advisor guide you. Don't worry or second-guess. Just stay the course.

10. Enjoy life!

CHAPTER 5
Advice on Advice

I hate painting. My wife has a great eye and the ability as an interior designer to put different colors, fabrics, and furniture together to create unique places to live, work, and play. She will pick out a color that she wants on a wall. A lot of decisions go into putting that color on the wall: Do you need oil-based, flat, or glossy paints? Do you paint the foot and toe molding the same color or different colors? What kind of paintbrush do you use? Do you use a rollover or spray painter? Do you use tape on corners? Simply put, for me to paint a closet would take me a week, and it would look like an amateur did it.

My wife and I have determined that for jobs we don't like to do or are not good at, it's best for us to hire someone so that we can concentrate our time, talents, and energy on the things we *are* good at.

Be honest with yourself: How many do-it-yourself projects have you done where you did a better job than a hired professional? I'm not asking whether you got better *value* by doing it yourself. I just want you to think about whether you're as good as or better than a pro, whether it's in remodeling your bathroom, selling your own home, preparing your own taxes, or defending yourself in court.

Now think about what is at stake in managing your finances. But first consider what I've already shared about the human tendency to be driven by irrational emotional reactions to market movements. Now let's consider how much you'll earn, save, and spend over the course of your life.

Say you earn an average of $100,000 a year during your career, over maybe 50 years of work. That's $5 million in total earnings. And then consider that during the following quarter century or more in retirement, you might have an annual income of $80,000 or more from Social Security, a pension, and/or retirement account withdrawals. Twenty-five times $80,000…that's another $2 million.

That's $7 million in all during your lifetime to save, spend, invest, give to charities, and/or pass on to the next generation. That's also $7 million in possible opportunity costs—things you might have done differently had you thought of it or had the discipline to do it better.

With stakes that high, maybe a little expert help would come in handy and be worth the investment. If you think you can stay on course and do better than a financial professional, despite having many other things on your to-do list and never having earned a degree or certificate in managing money or investing, then all the more power to you.

Of course, I am biased, as I earn my living providing financial advice. But I have also seen, as outlined throughout this book, the many ways in which smart, capable people can mess up and find their financial paths derailed one way or another just like I have painted some ugly rooms in my house.

I firmly believe that just about everyone can benefit from the hands-on advice of an unbiased, knowledgeable, experienced advisor. Even more so if that advisor is a fiduciary. *Fiduciary advisers* have a professional obligation to put their clients' interests ahead of their own. A fiduciary adviser has no conflict of interest and doesn't earn a commission or fee for selling any products. The adviser's interests are perfectly aligned with those of the client.

I'd like to point out the specific spelling of "adviser" here. I am using it in the context of the formal and legal "registered investment adviser," which indicates an adviser who has legal fiduciary responsibility to his or her clients. Elsewhere, throughout the book, we use the more common "advisor."

WHO COULD BENEFIT FROM FINANCIAL ADVICE?

Here are just a few brief scenarios where people in a variety of life stages or situations could benefit from financial advice:

- A young woman new to the workforce seeks guidance on how to budget, save, invest, and juggle financial priorities.

- A couple in their late 20s or early 30s is settling down to buy a home, raise a family, and plan their financial future together. They could use a financial blueprint.

- A middle-aged woman is about to begin anew after a divorce or the death of her partner. She might lack experience or interest in personal finances. She could gain from some guidance and reassurance.

- A pre-retiree is wondering how he or she will manage financially after the paycheck stops arriving. Can I afford to retire?

When should I take Social Security benefits? Which parts of Medicare do what? What is a safe systematic withdrawal rate? Should I consider a life annuity? What about an estate plan? There are lots of big questions to review with an expert.

I mentioned a few female-specific situations. That's because this book is geared to middle-class millionaire women. But the same can easily apply to men of all ages or in different stages of their lives. We're all emotional human beings who make mistakes with financial and other matters, so why not have a steadying hand to help keep us on track toward our goals, and to even help us formulate and articulate those goals?

YOUR PERSONAL CFO OR FINANCIAL THERAPIST

In my mind, a good financial advisor will think of him or herself as a chief financial officer, or CFO, for each of his or her clients. An advisor should consider each client as the chief executive officer, or CEO, of their personal finances. I'm not here to tell you what to do if you're undecided over a big financial decision. That decision should always be the client's to make. It could be whether to buy a beach house or a recreational vehicle (RV), or whether to buy a bigger or smaller primary residence.

A financial advisor should not be the one to say yes or no. Instead, the financial advisor should be the assistant who simply quantifies the financial pros and cons of what you, the client, are considering. An advisor should point out something that you hadn't thought of, such as the tax consequences, or some hidden costs you might not have considered—maybe your cash flow or some other things you're juggling financially. You get to make an informed choice, benefiting from your advisor's knowledge and advice.

My colleague Carol Petrov, also a financial advisor, uses a different analogy that also is relevant. She says our role "is almost like a therapist."

"Not all financial dilemmas are simple or have one right answer," she says. "So having an advisor who will listen to your concerns or help you work through various issues is important, especially for women. You should be able to have honest conversations and feel comfortable sharing your fears and dreams so that your advisor can help see you through them."

Here's an example of how we can provide value.

Time and time again, I see clients walk into our office with a concentrated portfolio of one or two stocks that make up half of their portfolio. The combination of Chevron and Exxon is not a diversified portfolio. Owning a few stocks is gambling. Owning a diversified portfolio is investing.

I also see people walk into the office with target-date mutual funds. As a matter of fact, 65 percent of retirement funds are defaulted into these one-size-fits-all funds. The problem with target-date funds is that the asset allocation is determined by just one variable: your age. It does not take into consideration whether your assets are taxable or nontaxable, the amount of your assets—$10,000 and $10,000,000 should have different asset allocations—or whether you are married or single, have no children or 10 children, or the interest-rate environment (1 percent or 10 percent interest rates). It takes more than just picking the right wall color to have a well-painted room. Having a thoughtful discussion with a professional advisor about your personal financial goals, risk tolerance, and other factors can figuratively, and potentially literally, yield dividends.

HOW TO FIND A GOOD FINANCIAL ADVISOR

There are a number of ways to find a good financial advisor. Most important is to be thoughtful and thorough so that you find the right advisor for you, someone whom you can trust and who specializes in what you want and need from an advisor.

You can start by asking around—maybe your good friends, family members, and professionals, such as an accountant or lawyer, might know and recommend someone. Word of mouth goes far in this business, which is highly personal and individual.

Once you have a few names, consider how each candidate earns their money. They may earn a commission, or they may be either a "fee-based" or "fee-only" advisor. Despite the similar-sounding descriptions, they have a fundamental distinction as to whether the recommendations come with some financial incentive. *Fee-only* financial advisors will have no conflict of interest, because they do not accept compensation of any kind from investment firms or insurance companies. Financial compensation can come in the form of a commission or mutual fund fee "trails," which is like a kickback for choosing one mutual fund over another. Many brokerage firm advisors operate under this type of structure, and it's nearly impossible to understand fully what you're paying them for their time, advice, and asset management.

Anyone who earns a commission for selling you a financial

product of some kind will have a potential conflict of interest. *Fee-based* advisors can earn some kind of commission or fee from a financial firm on top of the fees they charge you for managing your assets—known as an assets under management (AUM) fee—which is typically 1.0–1.5 percent. A fee-based advisor may also charge you by the hour for their service or charge a flat fee for a financial plan and then let you decide whether you want to buy their annuity or let them manage your investments for an ongoing fee.

On the other hand, *fee-only* advisors can tell you exactly what you paid them, as they typically charge you a percentage of the assets, such as 1 percent, which on a $1 million portfolio would be $10,000 per year. That might sound like a lot of money. But consider that the more *you* earn, the more *they* earn. Thus their interests are aligned with yours. Plus, most fee-only advisors consider themselves fiduciaries in that they conduct their business under a fiduciary duty to disclose any conflicts of interest and transparently show the fees their clients pay them.

The bottom line: Ask the prospective advisor, "How do you get paid?" Then you can decide for yourself what's most important and what suits your needs. If you don't have enough assets to have a fee-only advisor work with you, then at least you'll understand the nature of the relationship and value proposition so you can determine whether you get enough advice to make the commissions worthwhile. This is especially true if you're just starting to save and need life insurance as a new parent. Or perhaps you're getting ready to retire thanks to a pension and Social Security benefits but really don't have much else saved up and could use some long-term care insurance.

CREDENTIALS AND ETHICS MATTER

The world of financial advice giving is like an alphabet soup of credentials, which all sound quite similar and can be confusing. Consider one thing first: the CFP®, or CERTIFIED FINANCIAL PLANNER™, designation is considered the gold standard within the industry. Advisors must have a few years of experience, take an extensive course, and pass a six-hour exam to become a CFP®. They are held to strict ethical standards and must complete ongoing education. Other licenses and certifications that are relevant include Chartered Financial Analyst® (CFA®), Chartered Financial Consultant® (ChFC®), and Certified Private Wealth Advisor® (CPWA®), a relatively new designation for those who work with high-net-worth clients (over $5,000,000) and already have their CERTIFIED FINANCIAL PLANNER™ designation.

As for ethics, you definitely want someone who has a clean record and reputation before you allow them to guide you on your finances. You can check their records with the Financial Industry Regulatory Authority (FINRA), the Securities and Exchange Commission (SEC), and the CFP Board. FINRA makes it easy to learn about prospective brokers by looking them up on their BrokerCheck website. It's also good to see if they're members of associations such as the National Association of Personal Financial Advisors (NAPFA) or Financial Planning Association. Involvement in these communities shows you they are interested in bettering themselves through attending conferences or education sessions and networking with their peers.

KEY QUESTIONS TO ASK YOUR
PROSPECTIVE ADVISOR

Once you are ready to screen or interview a few prospects, meet with them and get a feel for who they are and whether you'd be comfortable working with them. Consider doing the following:

- Ask who is their ideal client. (Does that person sound like you? Are you a good fit?)

- Find out how long have they been practicing. You probably want someone with some experience or at least who works on a team.

- Engage them in a discussion about financial concepts, and get a feel for whether they can explain things simply and clearly to you.

- Ask how they might do projections on a retirement plan. If their assumptions seem reasonable and realistic, and maybe even a bit conservative, that's great. For example, a rate of return of maybe 6 percent a year on a diversified portfolio is a lot more achievable than 10 or 12 percent.

- Through all of this, ask yourself: Do they seem knowledgeable, client-focused, and trustworthy? Could you feel comfortable working with them? Chemistry is important. What does your gut instinct tell you?

- Finally, check their references.

THE FIDUCIARY STANDARD AND
WHY IT'S IMPORTANT

I can't emphasize enough the importance of working with a fiduciary fee-only adviser. You want someone on your side when managing your money. You want someone whom you can trust and who doesn't have a conflict of interest. That basically means: hire a fee-only fiduciary adviser if you have the chance.

ROBO-ADVISOR OR FULL-SERVICE ADVISOR?

You've heard the expression "You get what you pay for." Robo-advisors are like buying a wedding dress off the rack. They're low cost. Maybe you can't afford more. It might not be the exact style you want, but it'll do. But most wedding dresses need to be tailored to fit you just right, and this is especially important if you have a unique shape.

A full-service personal financial advisor, on the other hand, will provide a more personal, comprehensive, tailored experience. We're like your personal CFO or financial therapist. We know about finances, and we know about you. We'll listen to your concerns and address them. The choice is yours. But you get what you pay for, and if you have any complications like ongoing needs due to job changes, divorce, or the death of a family member, you'll benefit from having a full-service advisor, who will have more knowledge of your particular situation and be able to give you more tailored advice.

WORKING WITH YOUR ADVISOR

There are a number of ways that you can work with a financial advisor. The way that makes sense to us at Kendall Capital is to have a thorough, ongoing relationship that includes investment management but also takes into account a variety of other financial concerns, including saving for your children's or grandchildren's college education, saving for your own retirement, retirement income planning, estate planning, and gifting/philanthropic planning. In our view, how can you effectively plan for any one of these things without taking into account all of the others?

In summary, when looking for a financial advisor, take your time, do your homework, be thorough, and think about working with someone whom you trust and with whom you feel comfortable.

ONE FINAL PIECE OF ADVICE ON ADVICE: BE INVOLVED

If you are married or part of a couple, don't leave all of this to your partner or spouse. Be involved. Help find and select a financial advisor with whom you're both comfortable. Attend meetings with your financial professional.

One of you may be designated as "in charge" of this area of your lives. But the other partner should be aware, informed, and involved. Whether through death or divorce, marriages end. And women tend to outlive men. So, at some point, you could be the sole decision maker/CEO of your personal finances.

And you should be prepared to make good decisions all along.

We'll cover this some more in Chapters 10 and 13, "When Life Throws You a Curveball" and "Married and Not Fully Involved."

CHAPTER 6
Living Within Your Means

Spend less than you earn and you'll accumulate wealth over time. That's it. A short chapter. Thank you for your time.

Seriously, this isn't complicated. But sometimes things are easier said than done. We're tempted to spend. We're tempted to spend now. And we want to keep up with the Joneses. Of course, spending isn't a bad thing. Eventually, everything you earn will be spent, even if that's by the next generation or the one after that, assuming you're able and willing to leave a legacy.

So it's not about not spending money per se. It's about not spending too much too soon. We have to pace ourselves financially, just like a marathon runner needs to conserve energy throughout a 26.2-mile race to make sure he or she doesn't run out of energy. In our case, with money, we don't want to run out of money before we die. That's the topic of the next chapter: longevity.

But how we make sure our money lasts as long as we do means we can't outspend. Instead, we have to spend *less* than we earn. If you do that, over time you'll see your savings and your net worth grow and grow until one day you are able to retire and enjoy the fruit—and savings—of your labor.

So let's make this happen, in 10 simple steps. This isn't

rocket science, but you need a game plan, and then you need to follow it.

1. Know how much you earn and spend. What's your monthly (or yearly) salary? Look at your pay stub or your annual W-2 form. Multiply or divide appropriately to arrive at your monthly income. Put that number aside. Does that include your contributions to a retirement plan? Make note of that too. Now, how much do you spend each month?

2. Tally regular monthly bills. You can use your bank account statement as a fail-proof money tracker, but it helps a lot to break it all down. Start with your fixed expenses or fairly regular monthly expenses, like mortgage or rent; car loan or other personal loan payments; health insurance premium; utility bills, including electricity, heat, internet, cell phone...

3. Track smaller miscellaneous expenses. This will include things like groceries and dinners out, gas and other car expenses, and miscellaneous small items like that daily Starbucks coffee. Each time you spend money on these relatively small items, it might not seem like a big deal, but these expenses add up. It might help to track these smaller items for a few months and average out what you typically spend on them. In the end, your bank account balance doesn't lie.

4. Review your budget, and separate needs from wants. This is where you go from tracking or tallying to strategically deciding how you can spend less or spend differently. It's healthy to question your priorities. One good way is to separate items into "needs" and "wants." You might need to buy food. But you want to go out to dinner each week or several times a week. These discretionary expenses can be trimmed if you need to do so. That's much easier than trying to eat less food overall. I'm not advocating living a minimalist lifestyle and denying yourself pleasures and discretionary fun. But choose consciously whether those discretionary expenses make sense. Are you using that health club membership? Do you really need to go out to dinner three times a week? If you're an empty nester, could you benefit from downsizing?

5. Don't worry about the Joneses. Who are the Joneses anyway, and who cares what car they drive? Maybe you're into status. I'm not. But some people really want to look wealthy. I prefer to be wealthy. And the way I choose to do so is to drive a fairly reasonably priced car, and to drive it for quite a few years, rather than trading up to the latest model every three years or so. I've also lived in the same home for 20 years, not looking to upgrade every five years or so. Each time you move, it costs you money, lots of it. If you really want to keep up with those Joneses, at least be aware of how much money you're spending doing so, and also be aware of what other things you could be doing with that money.

6. Be smart and sensible with your money. Sometimes it's not about being stingy with yourself but spending your money wisely. I'll share an example about a client couple. They were Maryland residents who both worked for the federal government. They had a beautiful condo in Florida that they loved visiting. On average they spent two months, or 60 days, a year visiting their home away from home.

The problem was that the annual cost was quite prohibitive. The condo was worth $1.2 million, condo fees were $1,500 per month/$18,000 annually whether they used it or not, monthly utilities were $1,000/$12,000 annually, annual real estate taxes were $14,000, beachfront insurance was $15,000 per year, and their 5.0 percent mortgage on $1 million came to $50,000 in interest expense. The total annual carrying cost for this condo was over $109,000 per year whether they used it or not. If you broke down the annual cost, using the condo 60 days per year meant they were paying more than $1,800 per day for their time there.

Once I realized how much this was draining them financially, I suggested that they could sell the place, and for the same price while in Florida, they could stay in the executive suite at the Hyatt with room service. Turns out they didn't like that suggestion, so they fired me! Well, you can't win every time, but at least I shoot straight.

7. Pay off your credit card in full every month. This is admittedly easier for some of us than for others. But it's a good, essential financial housekeeping habit. Those credit card interest rates are just plain outrageous. And I believe that, other than the rare case when you just need to put something big on your card and you can't pay it off in one chunk, other than that *rare* case, you should never be in a position where you can't pay off your card balance in full every month.

8. *Build and maintain an emergency fund.* One surefire way to avoid those hefty credit card interest rates is to create an emergency fund that would cover three to six months of living expenses in an emergency. Let's say you lose your job and it takes you a few months to find another one. Or you incur a surprise medical bill or urgent home repair expense, such as flood damage, that more than depletes your bank account. You dip into that readily available emergency fund and take care of these emergencies without becoming a financial casualty yourself. And as soon as you've drawn from that fund, you begin to rebuild it for the next need.

The amount needed for an emergency fund will vary from person to person. Among the main considerations is the predictability of your income. Is your income a regular paycheck every two weeks from the federal government, for example, or does your income vary depending upon commission from sales? Are you the sole income earner in your household, or do you have two paychecks from different sources? However you get paid, set up your checking account to automatically transfer some amount to a savings account. Much like contributing to a retirement plan, you'll be earmarking some money before you have a chance to spend it. Then watch it grow in your savings account, and in no time you should have that emergency fund.

9. *Be a role model.* Set the right example for your kids. Nothing speaks louder than your own actions. If you want to raise financially responsible children, be a financially responsible adult. Share with them these techniques of disciplined savings and how to make thoughtful spending decisions.

10. Pay yourself first. I saved this one for last because it's the essential ingredient to continually growing your wealth over time, but before you can do it, you have to know that you are able to. You have to know that you are able to spend less than you earn. Once you do, earmark a set amount—perhaps 10 percent at a minimum, or 15 percent—of your salary to go into a saving account, such as a workplace 401(k) retirement savings plan or your own individual retirement account.

The reason I mention a range of 10–15 percent is that if you begin to save early enough in your career, you can actually save less overall because it will have more time to accumulate. If you wait a few years before beginning to save, you'll need to save more in order to catch up. Putting that money aside before you can see it will make saving and growing your wealth easy.

The good news: women are apparently better than men at being financially responsible. I know it's dangerous to make sweeping statements, and there are lots of examples of financially responsible and irresponsible individuals of both sexes. But a recent survey by Bank of America Merrill Lynch reported in the *Wall Street Journal* found that 41 percent of women said they would use extra disposable income to pay down debt, versus 36 percent of men. And just 14 percent of women said they'd use the money to buy more things, versus 19 percent of men.[5] So take a bow, women, if that's what *you* would do!

To summarize:

---

[5] https://www.wsj.com/articles/when-women-bring-home-a-bigger-slice-of-the-bacon-11565343002

1. Know how much you earn and spend.

2. Tally regular monthly bills.

3. Track smaller miscellaneous expenses.

4. Review your budget, and separate needs from wants.

5. Ignore the Joneses.

6. Be smart and sensible with your money.

7. Pay off your credit card in full every month.

8. Build and maintain an emergency fund.

9. Be a role model.

10. Pay yourself first.

Now that we have established how to save money, the next chapter will explain why it's absolutely essential—especially for women—to do this.

CHAPTER 7

Longevity: A Double-Edged Sword

O f all the risks out there, what could be greater than the risk of running out of money before you die? We tend to think of the rise and fall of the stock market, or volatility, when we think of investment risks, but it's actually the risk of outliving your money—*longevity risk*—because if you live so long and didn't save enough, that can be devastating.

Living a long life is great, as long as we're healthy enough to enjoy it, and as long as our finances are healthy enough to sustain us all the way through that long life. I won't tell you how to be physically healthy, because that's not what I get paid to do. But I will give you some pointers on how to prepare for a long, financially healthy life.

As you are likely aware, we are living longer and longer lives, far longer than our parents or grandparents did. The average life span for Americans born in 2019, based on the longevity calculator on the Social Security website, is 82.8 years for males and 86.7 for females.[6] As a comparison, life expectancy

---

[6]   https://www.ssa.gov/cgi-bin/longevity.cgi

in 1970, roughly a half century ago, was 67.1 for males and 74.7 for females.[7]

You get the picture. We're living longer overall, and women are living even longer than men. Making things more challenging for women is that despite some progress on pay equity, women overall still tend to earn substantially less than men, roughly 80 cents to the dollar.[8] Compounding *that* even further is that women often take some time out of the workforce—for example, when having a baby, raising a young family, or possibly when an aging parent or another close relative needs some care.

Put all those factors together and it's like women are climbing a mountain in high-heeled shoes. They had to start at sea level, while their male counterparts started at the base of the mountain. And along the way, they had to take really long pit stops, not because they needed them, but because others needed them to do so.

So how can we solve this longevity problem? Well, either simply don't live as long—which you can hardly control—or do everything you can to make your money last while retaining options in order to live with peace of mind and to stay in control. Here's how you make sure to get better shoes and make the most of your adventure while you're on your path to successfully conquer that mountain.

---

[7] https://u.demog.berkeley.edu/~andrew/1918/figure2.html

[8] https://nwlc.org/issue/equal-pay-and-the-wage-gap/

HOW DO WE MAKE OUR MONEY LAST?

1. Start saving early. By starting to save and invest for retirement at an early age, you'll give your savings more time to grow. Time is your friend when it comes to investing. Ideally, save at least 10 percent of your income. But even if all you can save is 5 percent of your income at first, do it! Of course, there'll always be some reason not to save for your future. When you're a young adult, even if you're really responsible financially, you might want to pay off student debt; save for a car or pay an auto loan; save for a wedding, a house, or a vacation; or simply keep up with basic monthly expenses.

But if you can manage to save some money early on and leave it alone to grow for decades, it can potentially grow enormously. And it's even better if you can keep saving steadily. We can illustrate the power of compounding with the help of the Rule of 72, mentioned in Chapter 3. It's a simple tool to show you how long it would take for money to double. By dividing 72 by an investment's annual rate of return, you'll see how many years it would take for money to double at that rate of return. For example, at a 3 percent annual return, it would take 24 years for an investment to double. But at a 9 percent return, it would double in eight years. Just divide any number into 72 and you'll see.

Taking this further, if you start early enough and invest aggressively enough that you have a higher potential return—for example, in stocks rather than conservative government bonds or certificates of deposit—your money will be able to double again and again and again. To see a specific illustration, skip ahead to #4: Invest for growth.

Let's look at Emily, who worked as a retail clerk and lifeguard during her high school and college years. Every year, her parents would contribute an amount equal to whatever she earned into a Roth IRA account in her name. At first it was just $1,000 or $2,000 per year, but when Emily graduated from college, her Roth IRA account had ballooned in value to over $15,000. After graduating from college, Emily "got it." She understood firsthand the concept of starting early and benefiting from compound growth.

Today Emily is 30 years old and makes her own contributions to aggressively save in her Roth IRA account. She does this regularly by paying herself first, contributing automatically from her paycheck to her employer's 401(k). At the ripe old age of 30, Emily's Roth IRA and 401(k) are worth more than $100,000. Using the rule of 72, we'll assume Emily's money will double in value every 10 years at a 7.2 percent rate of return.

Therefore, if Emily never contributes another dollar into her retirement accounts, they should be worth $200,000 when she reaches age 40, $400,000 at 50, $800,000 when she is 60 years old, and $1,600,000 when she reaches age 70. Not bad, considering it all started with her parents contributing a few bucks as a reward for working. Most importantly, though, this exercise was a terrific way to get Emily excited about saving and investing so that she knew exactly what to do when she got her first "real" job.

2. Save regularly—pay yourself first. The easiest way to find money to save is to make it impossible to spend. That means "pay yourself first," just like Emily did. In other words, put money away before you see it. Most employers can do that via automatic payroll withdrawal. That's easy and standard if you belong to a workplace savings plan like a 401(k) or federal government Thrift Savings Plan (TSP). But you can also arrange that for an individual retirement plan (IRA). You can't spend the money if you never see it!

3. Max out your savings. If you can participate in a 401(k) or similar workplace savings plan, try at least to save enough to receive the full employer match, if one exists. Often, contributing just 5 percent of your salary will give you the full "free money" match from your employer. You should also consider using the Roth 401(k) option if it's available to you while your income is relatively low. In addition to employer plans, you can also contribute to a Roth IRA if your income allows it.

But don't forget to save up that emergency fund. It's great to save for your long-term security, but realistically, you'll need money in the short term too. Think of it as different buckets. Your bank savings account needs a few drops of cash for short-term needs; your Roth IRA could use a few more drops because that money gets invested but *could* be used prior to age 59½.

I call it the *emergency* emergency fund because you can always take back contributions you've made without paying taxes or a 10 percent early-withdrawal penalty as long as you've had the account for at least five years. So open a Roth, even if you only put $100 in it to get started. Along with your employer-sponsored retirement plan, a Roth IRA will provide plenty of flexibility and opportunity for you to save for your future. Bottom line: save as much as you can by using a variety of tools.

4. Invest for growth. If you have a long investment horizon, such as a decade or longer, you should put a large portion of your diversified portfolio in growth investments, such as stocks and real estate. That potentially higher return can help your money grow faster. The impact of this growth can compound over long periods of time. And over a long period, you'll have time to ride out the market's highs and lows without having to access your savings. Most retirement plan providers will offer online resources to help you select a diversified allocation or model of mutual funds from across the investment spectrum.

Applying the Rule of 72, mentioned in point #1, let's assume that you have $10,000 to invest as a young adult straight out of school. In your early 20s, it's conceivable that you could let this sit for four decades or longer. If you invest it in a conservative investment that earns just 3 percent a year, over the course of 48 years, it would only double twice (once every 24 years; 72 / 3= 24). That $10,000 would double to $20,000 and double once more to $40,000.

Now, let's see how much your $10,000 would grow if invested at a steady 9 percent for 48 years—remember this is a hypothetical example, for illustration only. The $10,000 initially invested would double every eight years (72 / 9 = 8). Forty-eight years divided by 8 = 6, meaning that $10,000 would double six times:

Once: $20,000
Twice: $40,000
Three times: $80,000
Four times: $160,000
Five times: $320,000
Six times: $640,000

That difference between $40,000 and $640,000 will go a long way to resolving any concerns over longevity risk. Of course, in the real world, we invest regularly and steadily, not in a single chunk of $10,000. And returns aren't going to be steady. But the same principle of compounding over time will apply!

5. Dollar-cost averaging can help during ups and downs. Given that investment returns aren't always steady, there's a great way to benefit further from market downturns. That's through dollar-cost averaging. You invest the same dollar amount regularly, such as every pay period. When the price per share of the investment dips, you get to buy at a discount, buying more shares at a lower price per share. Over time, your dollar cost averages out, and you benefit from the periodic discounts that will happen when prices dip. Understanding this can help calm you during times of market volatility. Instead of panicking, you might see this as a silver lining.

6. Have a plan and follow it. Now that you see what's at stake, let's make a plan and put it to work. Set a goal. Save regularly toward that goal. Allow your savings to accumulate over time. That means steadily saving and not withdrawing from your long-term savings. Invest for growth, and monitor your progress. By participating in a workplace savings plan and saving regularly, you'll benefit from dollar-cost averaging, which means saving the same dollar amount at regular intervals. When the price of an investment rises, your dollar buys fewer shares, and when it dips, you buy more shares. That averages out the cost while instilling discipline.

7. Be conscious of expenses—trade less frequently. Generally, the more we trade investments, the more expenses we incur. As a rule of thumb, therefore, try to buy and sell investments less frequently. In addition, be mindful of fees and expenses, which can erode potential long-term investment earnings. By working with a fiduciary advisor rather than a commissioned salesperson, at least you won't be encouraged to buy products and pay commissions. Instead, you should be guided to invest wisely for your long-term goals.

8. If you take a leave of absence, power up savings on your return. In the real world, we don't necessarily enter the workforce straight out of school and remain there all the way until the day we retire. This is especially true for women. You may stop working for a few years along the way to raise kids, go back to school, take a sabbatical to travel, or help care for a sick relative. That means you won't be earning or saving money during that stretch. When you return to work, you may have many things competing for your financial attention. One thing to strive for is to power up your savings both before and after your leave of absence.

9. Keep your eyes on the prize. It's been said that saving for your retirement is a marathon, not a sprint. I'd correct that: it's actually an ultramarathon! It's a long financial journey, and along the way there will be countless competing money-spending necessities and desires. By performing regular annual personal financial reviews, you'll help yourself to stay on track and keep saving for your golden years.

10. Use tranches to protect your money. In my first book, *Middle-Class Millionaire*, I discussed the benefits of creating several segments or tranches of your portfolio focused specifically on the short term, medium term, and longer term. Each of these has a distinct purpose and investment focus. The short-term portion includes liquid (easy and quick to access), stable funds that can provide for your needs for a few years. The medium-term tranche provides income from bonds and dividend-yielding stocks that will augment your income as needed for up to a decade. Because both of those create an effective buffer against market volatility, you'll be able to invest the rest of your savings with a focus on long-term growth and higher potential returns.

11. Always include some growth investments. Working within the context of those tranches or tiers, because you have the basics covered for several years with more conservative investments, you can devote the longer-term part of your portfolio more heavily to growth. That's vitally important, because the key point of investing for a long-term goal is growth. You are able to take shorter-term market volatility in stride with little concern, because you will most likely not need to access this longer-term money for a long time. So invest for growth, with an emphasis on diversification.

12. Work longer to enhance your retirement years. As you get close to retirement, you can do a fairly accurate analysis of your retirement finances. Creating a thorough retirement budget is critically important, including the cost of health insurance, which encompasses Medicare and private supplemental coverage. Begin with your current expenses, and consider how they might change once you no longer work. Get into some level of detail so you have greater confidence in the findings. Estimate your sources of retirement income, including Social Security benefits and any pensions, then factor in how much you might need to withdraw each year from your retirement savings to make ends meet.

If you're not sure whether your money will last, you can play it safe for a year or two, or longer, and stay in the workforce a bit longer. For every year that you delay retirement, you'll be able to add to your nest egg, and you'll have one less year of retirement expenses to fund. And even if full-time work doesn't appeal to you, you could consider working part time.

Aside from earning more and saving more, many people also find that working longer can be highly satisfying and stimulating mentally and socially. Because we're living longer and many of us are healthy enough to work longer, it's becoming more common to delay retirement, and not just because people have to. They also want to.

Consider the case of a pediatric cardiologist I know who enjoyed his career. Soon after he retired, his health went down. There might or might not have been a direct correlation, but I know many cases where people's quality of life deteriorates when they are less connected to others socially and in the course of their daily routines.

13. *Defer Social Security benefits if you can.* I mentioned Social Security benefits as a key source of income. It's important to recognize the enormous control that you have over how great your benefits are each month and how much you'll receive over the course of your retirement. Your benefits are pegged at a so-called "normal retirement age" or "full retirement age" (FRA). That's the age when you will receive full benefits. Most people reading this book will have an FRA of age 67.

You have the option of taking your benefits as early as age 62 or as late as age 70. But for every year that you take them earlier than your normal retirement age, you'll receive smaller and smaller benefits, roughly 8 percent smaller benefits for each year before your full benefits would kick in, and you'll receive that smaller amount every month for the rest of your life.

Conversely, for every year that you delay your benefits, you'll receive monthly benefits of 8 percent more. So, if your full benefits would kick in at age 67, you could receive 24 percent more every month for the rest of your life just by waiting three extra years. If you think you'll live long enough to benefit overall from this delay—the breakeven age for waiting from age 67 to 70 is in the early 80s—then you're better off waiting.[9] So, if you're worried about outliving your money, this is a hugely important way to offset that risk.

14. *Withdraw from your retirement accounts at a sustainable rate.* It's widely accepted that for your retirement savings to last 30 or more years, generally considered a safe length of time to not run out of money in retirement if you stop working at roughly age 65, you should limit your withdrawals to 4 or 4.5 percent of your retirement savings in year one of retirement.

There's been some debate about this, and whether it could

---

[9]   https://www.fool.com/retirement/2019/09/21/how-your-social-security-break-even-age-affects-wh.aspx

be a bit higher or to what degree your asset allocation might influence that. But it's not a bad quick rule of thumb to work with. So, if you have $1 million saved, you'd want to withdraw no more than roughly $40,000 or $45,000 in your first year of retirement.

From that point on, you'll want to monitor how your retirement account balance is doing. It's helpful to recognize that our retirement expenses will tend to start a bit higher in our more active, healthy early days of retirement. By your 70s, you might be spending a bit less if you tend to stay close to home and travel less. And then by your 80s and beyond, medical bills might push up your costs. But that's where annual monitoring will help.

As I noted in *Middle-Class Millionaire*, I've found that retirees typically spend their first decade—ages 65–75—traveling and doing fun activities while they're healthy. By their 70s, they tend to spend more time going to exercise classes and their grandchildren's soccer games, so they simply aren't spending as much money as they used to. Once they reach age 85, they're more interested in watching *Judge Judy* or *Oprah* reruns on TV.

KEEP MONITORING AND ADJUSTING YOUR PLAN

Understand that longevity risk, like all aspects of financial planning, is not a one-and-done exercise. Stay on top of your finances. Monitor your financial picture regularly. Presuming that you work with a financial advisor, have a thorough annual checkup, just like you would with your family doctor. Then make adjustments as needed on your personal ultramarathon.

Circumstances that may warrant an adjustment include dramatic moves in the financial markets or changes to your health or family situation. So review your financial plan periodically to make sure you're on track and adjust as necessary.

CHAPTER 8
The Art of Financial Juggling

In an ideal world, you might have a single goal—financial or other—and be focused on achieving it before considering a second goal. That way you'd be sure of at least reaching that one goal, and then you'd take that success and build on it. But in the real world, we're always faced with more than one goal, and we can't afford to neglect something like retirement saving entirely in favor of saving for college tuition, for example. If we did that, we'd never get around to saving for our retirement.

LEARN FROM HOW YOU MULTITASK

Multitasking has become very common in our daily lives. How often are you doing something else while talking on the phone? Do you listen to podcasts while you drive? Do you read or respond to emails while drinking coffee or watching TV?

Some tasks do require your full attention, however. Driving while distracted could be fatal. And if I'm grilling meat, I want to be 100 percent focused, because if I get into an animated discussion, all bets are off as to whether that steak that was supposed to be medium rare is actually going to end up extremely well done, and by that I mean burnt. So multitasking might come at a cost in these situations.

So we *can* and *do* multitask in dozens of ways, with varying degrees of success. What does this mean for juggling financial goals? Let's take four common financial goals and see whether you can achieve success by tackling one at a time or trying to make progress on all of them at once or at least more than one at a time. I'm sure you might have your own top-four financial goals, but these four are commonly cited as critical.

I'm listing them here to make this discussion more concrete, and I'm doing it alphabetically so no one will think that retirement is less important than the other ones, because it should always be a top priority:

1. College savings
2. Debt payoff
3. Emergency fund
4. Retirement savings

If you chose to do one at a time, you might not be able to save for your retirement or for your children's college tuition until after you paid off your own debt and then established a six-month emergency fund. But in the process, you'd be losing time during which your early investment returns could potentially compound significantly.

DON'T IGNORE YOUR NEEDS

One problem I tend to see with women is they will often put the needs of others before themselves. I have seen women time and time again put money into college saving while making minimum monthly payments to high-interest credit card accounts or even their own student loan debt. This is not advisable, especially when the cost of debt is 10, 12, or even 18 percent, while the expected rate of return for most college savings plans is much lower. To see the heavy cost of waiting, look back at the Rule of 72, mentioned in Chapters 3 and 7.

From a financial perspective, the real issue—for men and women—is what to do with that additional dollar of earnings. As we have previously mentioned, the first thing all middle-class millionaire women need to do is establish that emergency fund, the size of which can vary widely depending upon the predictability of your income and characteristics of your debts. For example, if you work for the federal government and have a predictable paycheck every two weeks, you'll need a smaller emergency fund than a woman who works as a commissioned salesperson and who might go months without earnings.

Your debts and their characteristics will also affect how much you'll need in an emergency fund. For example, if you have a strong credit score, an unused home equity line of credit, and zero-balance credit cards, your need for emergency funds will be less than a woman with a low credit score, tapped-out line of credit, and maxed-out credit cards.

YOUR PERSONAL MARGINAL COST OF CAPITAL

Once you've funded your emergency fund, as mentioned before, the next question is what to do with the additional dollar earned. Most women should look at their personal balance sheet for the cost of the highest debt they owe; that rate will determine your personal "marginal cost of capital." If you have a credit card that costs you 15 percent, then 15 percent will be your personal marginal cost of capital.

You should view your personal marginal cost of capital as your personal hurdle rate. If you cannot make more than your personal marginal cost of capital, then spend your next investable dollar to pay down that 15 percent debt, because saving a dollar is as good as, if not better than, investing a dollar. But when the marginal cost of capital debt is at 3, 4, or even 5 percent, you need to analyze the benefits of contributing to retirement accounts that offer the initial benefits of saving on federal, state, and local taxes. That is 22 percent federally for single filers with taxable income between $38,700 and $82,500, and it jumps to more than 24 percent for filers with taxable income above $82,500.

In many states, the combined state and local taxes can add 5–10 percent more. Now, I think borrowing money with our right hand at a personal cost of marginal capital at 4 or 5 percent and making an investment with our left hand that initially saves a combined 30 percent makes great sense, and I'd advise middle-class millionaire women to do that all day long.

TAX-FREE RETIREMENT SAVINGS GROW FASTER

Let's return to the tendency for many women to think of others first—and if they have children, their first concern is the children's college education. But the math makes sense in most cases for the woman to build up her retirement accounts first and then save for her children's college education. Simply put, saving in your retirement account allows your money to grow tax-free and therefore faster. Depending on your total financial picture, you could pause or lower your retirement account contributions for a few years as your child enters college. Your children will demonstrate more of a financial need if you have most of your financial assets in a retirement account rather than a taxable or college saving account. So you won't pay a price for having those savings.

However, even though it makes sense mathematically to put as much in retirement savings as you can before starting a college savings plan, emotionally that can be hard to reconcile. We understand that, and that's where juggling comes into play. Consider saving at least enough to get the company match on your 401(k). Then, if you're eligible, make the maximum contribution to a Roth IRA. Roth IRAs offer more flexibility for withdrawals, and they can be used for educational expenses without penalty.

529 COLLEGE SAVINGS PLANS ARE GREAT TOOLS

But if you want to dedicate a separate account for college, the 529 plan is the way to go. Start with your state's plan if you want to get a state tax deduction on your contributions, and set up the account for automated contributions. Many plans can start with as little as $25 per month! Don't feel bad if you can't save the amount that your financial planner says is necessary to fully fund a college goal. We're juggling, remember? But you'll feel better knowing you've at least started an account and are doing the right thing. Then, as your income increases and debts get paid off, increase that monthly amount.

I'm reminded of some clients who came to us in their 40s. I was so impressed at the fact that they had already accumulated quite a bit in their 401(k) plans, and they shared how they live within their means, but because the cost of day care was a killer, they couldn't save as much as they used to before they had kids. They started 529 plans at the behest of their parents, who wanted to contribute birthday and holiday gifts to their grandkids.

At least they were managing to keep debts down, and they used their bonuses to replenish their cash reserves that they had spent on home repairs. They were doing a great job of juggling, and now that their youngest was in elementary school, they knew exactly where to save those dollars they used to spend on day care. They returned to maximizing their 401(k)s and making significant contributions to their 529 plans.

Admittedly, financial juggling can be a challenge. Here are some tips to consider:

Set priorities and commit to them. Pick a top priority. First think about what you want to accomplish financially, and select a single *top priority* goal. This isn't the only goal you'll have, but you will place it above the others. Then fund it by having money automatically taken from your paycheck or your bank account regularly to pay off that high-interest debt, fund your retirement, or establish an emergency fund.

Identify one or two more secondary goals. These might not get as much money or attention as your top priority, but make a point of setting those goals and creating an action plan on each one. And when you do a thorough financial review—at least once a year and possibly more frequently, such as quarterly—check on your progress toward each one.

Create separate accounts. Earmark separate accounts for each specific goal. This is important so that you can track your progress toward each separate goal. It's also a way to reinforce your commitment to that individual goal. Every time you look at your investment statement, you'll think of what that money is being saved for, whether it's for retirement, college, or emergency cash.

Also, each goal should have its own time line, which will influence what type of investments you use to reach that goal. If your retirement is decades away, that means you can afford to invest more aggressively—in other words, primarily in stocks. But the purpose of an emergency fund is to always be available for immediate possible use. That means using conservative, safe, and lower-yielding investments. So create a separate savings account, and schedule monthly transfers of some amount after your paycheck is deposited and your bills have been paid. Another way to view this account is as "cash reserves." Once you've established a baseline of, say, three to six months of living expenses, you could use this cash for things like a weekend getaway with friends or an enriching summer camp experience for your child. When faced with the temptation to spend on things you don't need, it helps to ask yourself, "Do I really want to pull money from my savings for this?" It gives you a moment of pause and makes it easier to pass on buying that item.

Monitor your progress in your annual personal financial review. An annual personal financial review should be part of your routine no matter what your goals for a variety of reasons. When you have specific financial goals, reviewing your progress each year is a perfect way to chart your progress.

Work with a financial advisor. No matter what your financial situation or your particular goals, working with a fiduciary financial advisor—who is committed to serving your best interests—can help you realize that goal. It will provide discipline, which we all need to some degree, and guidance. For some of us, when the market gets more volatile than usual, it can be reassuring to have an experienced, objective advisor to calm us down and in some cases "talk us off the ledge," so to speak, and to keep us on track. A financial advisor may also see opportunities to use some existing assets more efficiently. For example, you might not want to sell some stock that your grandmother gave you because of the 15 percent capital gains tax. However, using it to wipe away a big credit card bill or pay for a wedding may be your best option.

A recent study by Vanguard Investment Management noted that true independent fee-only advisors add roughly 3 percent value per year.[10]

Don't neglect retirement savings. It's been said before, but it's so important that it deserves to be repeated: never neglect your retirement savings. It's truly the most important financial goal

---

[10] https://www.vanguard.com/pdf/ISGQVAA.pdf
https://kendallcapital.com/measuring-the-value-of-a-financial-advisor/

you will ever have. Other goals will certainly crop up, including major ones, such as college savings. While it's natural and good to want to help your kids or grandchildren financially, that should only be done as a complement to your number one goal, which is to make sure you're going to be financially secure by the time you reach your retirement. There's no financial backstop or safety net for your retirement beyond Social Security benefits, which will only go so far. You can't take out a loan to pay for retirement, but your kids *can* do that to pay for their college expenses.

The desire to help or nurture others is a beautiful thing, but if you neglect your own retirement savings in the process, you actually risk becoming a financial burden on your children at a certain point. That's surely not what anyone I know wants for themselves or their children.

Don't ignore that emergency fund or cash reserves. No matter how many other financial goals you have, the presence of an emergency fund can actually help you meet those other goals. That's because if an emergency happens, being able to handle that temporary financial adversity with a source of money earmarked for that purpose means that you won't need to touch those other investment accounts dedicated to separate goals. Once you've saved enough to cover potential emergencies, such as car repairs, replacing appliances, and being laid off from your job, keep building up your nonretirement savings. It can open up opportunities to get another degree or move to another city for a fresh start. Remember, having a savings account will provide you with options and flexibility when you need them.

Progress steadily. The commitment to a goal and the use of automatic savings features can be enormously effective. But in real life, sometimes stuff happens that can get in the way. Maybe there's a job loss or a divorce. You might have to tighten your belt and suspend your retirement savings contributions if things get really tight. But always try and make forward progress toward your number one goal, even when finances get a bit tight.

Keep learning about finances. Continue to learn about how to manage your money, and keep striving to improve your personal financial management. Always seek to become more confident, capable, and empowered. This is important for you, obviously, but also for your children.

Whether you or they realize it, you are a very important role model as their mother. And becoming self-reliant financially will likely help them as well one day. As part of this, explain to your kids at an early age that they'll be responsible for at least a portion of their college savings. This will help set realistic expectations and teach self-reliance. We'll get into more detail on this in Chapter 14, "Raising Financially Savvy Children." Finally, as much as I have emphasized certain things, such as the importance of saving for retirement, there are many possible financial paths. So chart and follow your own path. And enjoy the journey!

SECTION III

One Size Doesn't Fit All

This book is about addressing the varying financial needs and interests of women and providing the information and tools for you to succeed financially through life. It's understood that women's situations can't be generalized into a single size that fits all. In this section, Chapters 9–13, we address a variety of situations or themes that might apply to some women but won't affect others.

CHAPTER 9

You Do It Your Way

Like so many things in life, there is no guaranteed or ideal financial path to follow, especially regarding women and their personal financial goals. To begin with, everyone is different. We all have our own situations, goals, and preferred ways to go about trying to reach those goals.

On the other hand, we all need guidelines as to how we could get from point A to point B in life and with regards to our personal finances. Ben Franklin famously said, "In this world nothing can be said to be certain, except death and taxes." I would add one more near-universal certainty to that: you need to save for your retirement, because unless you are born wealthy and know for certain that you'll be financially carefree at age 60 or 70, you do have to put some money away.

Beyond the trio of certainties—that we will die one day, that we will have to pay taxes along the way, and that we will have to save some money for our retirement—you have a fair bit of say over just about everything else in life.

Some questions to consider include:

- *How will you earn money?*

- *How will you save and invest your money?*

- *What will your financial priorities be?*

- *If you are in a long-term relationship, how will you and your partner or spouse decide to manage your household finances?*

- *How much money will you give to charities, and what types of charities will you support?*

WOMEN ARE MORE DIVERSE IN THEIR GOALS THAN MEN

Generally speaking, women tend to be less numbers oriented than men. A lot of personal finance books are written from or for a man's perspective. That includes more of a linear approach to life and continual approach to careers along with how we earn, spend, and invest money. For men, financial success is often equated with the earning of money or accumulation of funds. These can be summed up by the answers to standard questions such as "How much do you earn?" or "What's your net worth?"

Women, in my experience and from what I have read, are less likely to focus on accumulating money as a goal in and of itself. Instead, they're generally more inclined to see money as a tool or a way to reach a goal, which will have greater personal meaning.

Money can represent the freedom to do various things, such as travel, take time from work, or live a certain lifestyle. And that freedom is often applied to nurturing types of activities or concerns rather than a more self-indulgent approach. Quite often, and much more often than men, women will take deliberate breaks from the workforce or from full-time employment to give birth to and raise children or to care for family members, such as elderly or infirm parents.

Some people might call this more of a values-driven approach. I think it's more reflective of one size not fitting all, especially in today's world and especially when it comes to women, what they want from life, and how they choose to get there. For many women, *saving for retirement* is a less meaningful goal than *achieving financial independence* or *being financially stable*. It's that drive for stability that amazes me sometimes. Women often have to work harder and make greater sacrifices to get ahead than men.

Take for example one of our clients, Susan. She married young, had a couple of children in quick succession, and then soon realized she was in a dangerous situation. Her husband became abusive and couldn't hold down a job. Susan knew she had to make a change, but she was fiercely independent and didn't want to move back in with her parents. They already had enough on their plate taking care of her younger siblings. So she explored her options and found a nursing program in another state 1,200 miles away that was offering full scholarships. She packed up her car with her kids and filed for divorce.

Getting set up in a new town wasn't easy. Between her school schedule, working part time, and taking care of her children, she was exhausted. She also had to swallow her pride and accept some welfare and subsidies, a necessity because her ex-husband was unemployed. But she persevered and earned a master's degree on a scholarship. "After all," she said, "why stop at being a registered nurse when you can earn more with a master's degree?" Talk about being values driven!

Susan had a terrific career and raised two successful children, and although she could afford to retire now, she is still driven to work and save money to avoid the risk of becoming a burden on her kids someday. In the meantime, she loves being able to help her children get ahead by helping with a house down payment or helping save toward her grandchildren's college.

In a 2018 study by the investment firm PIMCO, "Women, Investing and the Pursuit of Wealth-Life Balance,"[11] 84 percent of women who were surveyed said they saw investing as a tool for creating life choices. That rises to 90 percent for women with $100,000 or more in investable assets.

A tool for creating life choices. I like the sound of that. Investing is there to facilitate progress along your path and help you reach your goals, whatever they are. Some women aren't that different from men in how they approach life, particularly if they don't choose to start a family. But many are different and have a wide variety of goals, aspirations, and paths through life.

You might place a high priority on saving for your children's college. Traveling extensively might be high on your bucket list. Living in a particular kind of community where you feel you belong might appeal to you strongly, to the point that you're willing to sacrifice in other ways in order to afford that. Some women place a very high priority on philanthropy and volunteering, giving to others in a variety of ways.

---

[11] https://www.pimco.com/en-us/our-firm/diverse-perspectives/wealth-life-balance/

For many women, investing is part and parcel of that values-driven approach to life. The terms socially responsible investing (SRI) and corporate social responsibility (CSR) have become increasingly popular. Under these investment categories, investors seek to support and invest in organizations that strive to "do good and do well," to quote one commonly used phrase.

Only you can decide on your path, but applying the time-tested and financially responsible middle-class millionaire approach to handling your finances will help you to have the means to realize your goals.

For example, you might choose to take some time from your career, and while you recognize that you'll pay some kind of financial price—for example, in the opportunity cost of passing up some period of full-time earnings—you're willing to do so. At the same time, however, you know you'll have to make up the difference in a variety of ways. You might tighten your belt financially, if you need to, or be willing to work part time in retirement.

There are many potential trade-offs. Being equipped with a good financial plan, a tool kit of sorts, will help you make your goals a reality. And that sounds like success to me, without putting a number on it.

CHAPTER 10

When Life Throws You a Curveball

We do our best to plan for the future, but often we are ill prepared when life actually throws us a big curveball, or perhaps we could call it a gut punch. I'm talking about big setbacks, such as a divorce or the death of a spouse. No matter how in control we might seem to be until something like that changes our world, an abrupt change can shake everything up. The toll can be felt in many ways—emotionally, socially, and financially.

The good news is that these major life changes are common, and people do carry on. This chapter is devoted to helping you do so as smoothly as possible. First, if you are reading this while going through some turmoil, my deepest sympathies. These are tough times, so aside from having to take care of business, be sure to take care of yourself. Allow yourself time and space to grieve, and don't be in too much of a rush to get everything done ASAP. Take it one day at a time, and tackle one thing at a time.

It's true that the net impact of divorce and widowhood are largely similar in that they involve the loss of a life partner. But let's look at each one separately, because there are obvious and important differences in terms of how you need to respond to each of these life-changing events.

DIVORCE: RECOVER, REGROUP, AND REJUVENATE

You've probably heard or read that one in two marriages ends in divorce. That might not make your divorce easier to deal with in the moment, but for what it's worth, you have lots of company. Here are some other interesting statistics:

The U.S. divorce rate has declined somewhat in recent years, but it remains close to 50 percent, with roughly 41 percent of first marriages ending in divorce, 60 percent of second marriages, and 73 percent of third marriages.[12] Interestingly, while rates of divorce have dropped among younger people, they've risen sharply among baby boomers.

According to a study by the National Center for Family and Marriage Research,[13] the rate of divorce for those under age 24 has dropped by 43 percent. A key factor is that young couples are cohabiting more than in the past, and this is allowing them to "try on" their mate before making a commitment. The divorce rate for 25–34 year olds has also dropped significantly, either because couples are waiting to become more financially stable

---

[12]   https://www.wf-lawyers.com/divorce-statistics-and-facts/

[13]   https://www.wsj.com/articles/the-divorce-rate-is-at-a-40-year-low-unless-youre-55-or-older-11561116601

or, again, they're living with a mate or two before committing to one for life.

However, the divorce rate for 35–54 year olds has stayed roughly the same. This is the age group where we see the most financial disruption. Within this group, we see two kinds of divorcees: the ones with young children and those with "done" children, meaning the kids have gone off to college or otherwise left the nest, leaving the parents without the glue that held their marriage together.

We've also noticed an increase of divorcees in their late 50s and early 60s. As it turns out, the divorce rate for this cohort has nearly tripled in recent years. This so-called "gray divorce" has left some women stunned that their husband would divorce them at this stage of the game. But fortunately, these women tend to have the resources to live comfortably. They just need help from wealth advisors to feel empowered and understand their financial situation.

And according to AARP research, two-thirds of women over age 40 who go through a divorce say they initiated it. Only 14 percent of women going through a mid- to late-life divorce say they were caught off guard, compared with 26 percent of men. So maybe this isn't quite the big curveball that many perceive it to be.

DOING DOUBLE DUTY LEAVES LITTLE TIME FOR A CAREER

Every divorce has a story, and our clients often come to us at a time when they've recently finalized the settlement and they need a friendly, supportive financial coach. Take for example Judy, our stay-at-home mom from Chapter 1.

Judy has been out of the workforce for 15 years, and she has three kids who do several activities to which she dutifully chauffeurs them while trying to squeeze in meal preparation and homework help. Her chauffeuring duties start at 3:00 p.m., making it impossible for her to take a full-time job. While her ex-husband pays her alimony, and they agreed that keeping the kids engaged with these activities is most important, financially speaking, she's behind the eight ball, because she's expected to work for her own spending money. However, between dropping off her youngest at 9:00 a.m. and picking up her oldest at 3:00 p.m., she's limited in the types of jobs she can do and the amount of income she can earn.

I certainly appreciate what Judy does, as I've watched my wife do the same thing for years. I can also empathize with her conundrum and understand that for her, regrouping and rejuvenating after her divorce may take a few years as she waits until her children are able to drive themselves to practices and games.

According to the U.S. Government Accountability Office, women's household income dropped by 41 percent post-divorce after age 50, while men's household income fell by 23 percent. Women clearly take the bigger hit financially, because in many cases a man will earn more than his wife. So, if you're not part of a dual-income home like Judy, these sobering statistics point to the importance of having your financial house in order when you get divorced.

For example, you should always have your own checking or savings account, especially if you're earning an income. Not only is it important for you to reap the benefits of your hard work, this is your first line of defense if you feel an impending divorce. One client told me she felt trapped when she realized that there was no account with her name on it that she could access without her husband finding out. How could she pay a lawyer for a consultation in the first place? It was terrifying for her and made her feel powerless.

CHECKLIST: 13 THINGS TO DO POST-DIVORCE (OR BETTER YET, START DOING BEFORE THE DIVORCE)

Here are a baker's dozen things to do after a divorce. Some of them might seem obvious, but they're important to take note of and take care of.

1. Cancel all joint accounts. If you don't do that, you're opening yourself up to the risk of an unpleasant surprise, such as unexpected charges on credit cards that you might be on the hook for.

2. Change beneficiaries and retitle assets in your name. Remember to change beneficiaries on every single financial account you own. Otherwise you might be unintentionally generous with your ex-spouse when you pass. So take your time and be thorough when changing beneficiaries in your IRA, 401(k), and life insurance policy unless your divorce agreement dictates that you need to keep your ex-husband as the recipient of some life insurance. If you jointly owned your home but now received it as part of your settlement, make sure it is retitled *in your name only* post-divorce. These are not-so-little details with big consequences if not done right.

3. Update all your insurance coverage. You are embarking on a new life on your own now. Review all your insurance coverage (health, long-term care, property, disability, life) and make sure it's what *you* need and want moving forward.

4. Meet with an estate attorney. I know, I know: the last thing you want to do is pay another attorney's fee. However, after divorce, it's important to reevaluate your assets and desires for how those assets are to be passed on if you suffer an untimely demise. The estate attorney will also tell you if you should have a revocable living trust and how to leave any assets to your children. These are answers you'll need as you update your beneficiaries with various financial institutions. It also comes into play when retitling your home.

There's another very important reason to meet with an estate attorney, and that's to help you plan for an unexpected health emergency. In the event that you were to become injured in an accident and unable to make decisions for yourself, it's now more important than ever to have someone legally named as your medical power of attorney as well as financial power of attorney. You can choose a friend or family member for either or both roles, but make sure you have your choices documented. Your financial advisor can also help by simply using forms to update existing accounts.

5. Check your credit score and begin to build your own credit history, solo. Check your credit score as you go through your divorce. If you see any errors or issues, report them immediately so they don't adversely affect your ability to obtain a loan, insurance coverage, or apartment rental. If you never had a chance to build up your own credit history, it might be prudent to apply for new credit cards before you cancel a joint credit card account. Building your own credit history will happen over time, but recognize that this is a critical time to be financially responsible and to begin to build a positive post-divorce credit history.

6. Protect your income. Now that you'll head a single-income household, consider buying disability insurance just in case you get injured or ill and are unable to work for a period of time. You can always cancel this coverage down the road, but at this critical time, protect yourself and your family.

7. Create a new financial plan. Any major life event is a good reason to review your financial plan. And there aren't too many life events that are more significant than a divorce. Take your time. And take charge. Be thorough, and consider everything from a new lens. This includes reviewing your financial goals, tolerance for risk, asset allocation, and estate plan. You may have new opportunities—including contributing to a Roth IRA—that you didn't have before based on your joint income.

8. Set up a new budget. This is part of your financial plan, but I want to highlight it because it's such an essential nuts-and-bolts piece of your financial health. If you're in control of your monthly income and expenses, good things will flow from that. Speaking of flow, focus on your cash flow. Life will probably throw some surprises at you in the first year or two post-divorce, and having some free cash available will help you take those surprises in stride.

9. Create an emergency reserve fund. This might be a bit challenging in the early days post-divorce, as you will undoubtedly find yourself spending money on some one-time purchases to replace items such as furniture or a car that your ex-spouse takes. But it should be a high priority. So tighten your belt if you can, and set aside whatever you can to build your emergency fund. You will thank yourself for it later.

10. Run new tax projections. Pay a visit to your CPA. This exercise will be helpful as part of your new financial plan, and it will help ease any surprises come tax time in the year following your divorce. This also might affect how you invest, but at the very least make sure things like your estimated taxes or tax withholding is as accurate as possible.

11. Avoid well-meaning unsolicited advice. Because divorce is so common, you're likely to hear all kinds of advice from friends and family, nonexperts who probably mean well or might feel a need to unburden themselves about things they went through. Pay little heed to these bits of advice, relying instead on the professionals.

12. Rely on your trusted circle of advisors, including your lawyer, financial planner, and accountant. They are the pros who know what they're talking about and who have, or should have, your best interests at heart. They can also be great sounding boards. I'm reminded of Barbara, who was referred to us by her father after her divorce. Her kids were fully launched, and her company was looking for long-term employees to take early retirement. As she was in her mid-50s, she knew she couldn't live off her retirement account without incurring the 10 percent tax penalty, but without alimony, she needed to stretch her severance payment as long as possible, and she was concerned that it would take time to find a new job at this stage in her career.

Fortunately, we were able to take advantage of a special tax-friendly rule called a qualified domestic relations order (QDRO) that we'll discuss in detail later, and she devised a budget she could live with, allowing her to enjoy her "sabbatical" from work. This time off helped her recover from the shock of divorce, regroup, reflect on her career potential, and rejuvenate. It was critical that she had the time and resources to spend with her children and friends. I'd like to think that having our support and learning about the financial tools available to her helped alleviate her stress and allowed her to enter this next chapter of her life with confidence.

13. Take control. You are in charge now. This is an opportunity for you to flex your freedom muscles and to become more knowledgeable and self-sufficient. It might seem daunting at first, but it can be empowering. Consider taking a course in managing your personal finances. Or just read books and articles and visit financial websites, looking up relevant topics and becoming more adept over time.

NEW OPPORTUNITIES AFTER DIVORCE

The fact that two out of three mid- to late-life divorces are initiated by women tells me a couple of things. First, women are taking charge of their lives, which is a great thing. Also, there appear to be a lot of unhappily married women. While that is sad, the flip side is that, apparently, there may be a large number of happily divorced women.

With that in mind, let's look at some of the opportunities that can arise from divorce. I'm not advocating divorce, just sharing some things that might paint a sunnier or more balanced picture. After all, if you have some lemons, why not make lemonade?

1. Gaining control and financial freedom. Money matters are often a source of tension in a marriage and may lead to divorce. If you and your spouse had key differences over financial priorities, post-divorce you might breathe a big sigh of relief and enjoy doing your own thing without that marital tension anymore. This theme of gaining financial freedom and control over your finances after divorce makes me think of the Rolling Stones song "Under My Thumb." I also recall a particular case involving a successful professional whom I'll call Pamela. Because she was busy with her career and raising three children, she let her husband take care of all the investment decisions while she helped the kids with their homework and took care of the house.

When they went through the divorce, she needed a real-life crash course in understanding their investments: What type of accounts did they own? Were they liquid? What was the tax impact of liquidating them? It was a lot to comprehend during a time of emotional stress, and she really wished she had paid more attention. All of that quick learning and financial catching up added to her stress.

But there was a silver lining. Pamela's husband had been quite controlling and always told her no when she wanted to spend money. It didn't matter that she had a substantial income and contributed handsomely to their financial accounts. She was still restricted from spending or giving money the way she desired, whether it was for a vacation with the kids, to help them buy a car, or even to make a charitable donation to a cause she believed in!

This disparity in their values was a major strain on the marriage. And it was one factor that led her to decide to divorce him. There she was, a hardworking woman, successfully raising children, and she didn't want to spend the rest of her life hoarding money and not enjoying any of it!

As we discussed her post-divorce financial plan, we were able to show Pamela how financially secure she was, aside from helping her understand and navigate the various types of accounts and investments so she could feel more in control of her savings. Because she was now on her own, with greater financial freedom, once we were able to assure her that she could afford to enjoy those family vacations and give to worthy causes, with a big sigh of relief, Pamela finally took her first trip to Europe with her children!

2. Penalty-free early access to your retirement fund. I have mixed feelings about this, but it's important to point out. If your settlement consists primarily of your ex-husband's retirement plan and you need cash to live on until you can find a good job, then you should know that you can access these funds before age 59½ without paying a penalty. It's called a qualified domestic relations order (QDRO) and is a way for your ex-husband to give you a portion of his 401(k) or other retirement plan without a taxable distribution occurring. Essentially, you now have an account with his 401(k) plan provider in your name, and you would pay the taxes on any money distributed. So, while you want to be mindful of how much you withdraw in a given year, at least you won't be penalized as you would in the case of withdrawals from an IRA or your own 401(k) account. This is a special type of account solely available to divorcées. So, before anyone recommends rolling over your QDRO to an IRA, please be sure that you do not have an impending need for income if you're under age 59½.

Another little-known way to access penalty-free retirement dollars is through a Roth IRA. If possible, you should negotiate to receive Roth IRA assets in a settlement, because not only are the distributions tax-free after age 59½, if you're under 59½, you can withdraw principal (the amount contributed over the years) without owing any tax or penalty.

3. More college financial aid. This is definitely a rose-colored-glasses-type view, but because money will likely be somewhat tighter, you could qualify for more financial aid through the Free Application for Federal Student Aid (FAFSA). I won't get too far into the weeds here, but be sure to study the details about custodial and noncustodial parents and potentially structure a favorable settlement that will lead to a good outcome on eligibility for financial aid.

4. Potentially better investment returns. Some women feel out of their element in the world of investing. But the flip side is that many men are too sure of themselves, to the point of taking too many risks or ill-advised ones. I'm sure there are plenty of stories that could illustrate both sides here. But many women will do well on their own as investors just by being prudent and cautious investors, and by being more receptive than men to receiving financial advice from their investment advisor or financial planner. Just try and avoid the tendency to be overly conservative.

WIDOWHOOD: A TIME OF MAJOR TRANSITION

While divorce can sometimes be a time of relief and rebirth, widowhood typically will take a longer and heavier emotional toll. Accept that, and give yourself time to heal and transition. Also, be ready to lean on others, at least in the initial period after you lose your partner or spouse. As with divorce, widowhood comes with its own story. There are women like Peggy from Chapter 1, who found herself a widow in her early 60s when her husband died in an accident. They were on top of the moon, having just married off their last child, and they were ready to plow their incomes into paying off that wedding and other bills that had accumulated while they paid for four college tuitions. Peggy and her husband also had a large mortgage and used up their home equity line of credit over the years.

She knew they were stretched thin, but the plan was to work another 10 years anyway because they both loved their careers and earned good incomes. But her husband slipped and fell, causing a brain injury from which he could not recover. Peggy was devastated, but fortunately, she had a good friend who referred her to us, and we helped her organize her financial affairs, which her husband had handled, and we helped her formulate a strategy.

Peggy's biggest regret was letting her husband cancel the term life insurance policy, which had become more expensive when he turned 60. That's what these policies do: they're cheap for 20 or 30 years, and then they become expensive and people don't like to pay for them. However, when you have as much debt as Peggy and her husband had in their 60s, having that $1 million life insurance payout would have meant Peggy could pay off the mortgage and home equity line of credit as well as all of the credit card bills. Sure, she had some other insurance on him through her employer, and that helped to give her breathing room and clear some debts, but she now had no choice but to keep working full time in order to pay the mortgage and upkeep on the big family house. Having it paid off would have given her the option to ease into retirement at a point in her life when her job, while rewarding, was becoming physically taxing.

Here's a checklist of immediate actions to help any recent widow, along with some longer-term financial concerns. As with the divorce checklist, it helps to understand these items before you're in a crisis. One point that I can't repeat enough is to review the beneficiaries on all retirement accounts and insurance policies regularly. There is nothing worse than finding out that your husband forgot to list you on his 401(k) account and the default is his estate. This is a costly mistake that I see over and over again. It's almost as bad as the times I see someone's ex-wife still listed as a beneficiary on such an account.

Back to the task at hand: think of this as a guideline, but if you have a financial advisor, I would recommend calling them first so they can help give you a specific to-do list.

1. Notify all financial institutions. Collect all statements of assets, and notify the firm that handles those assets. If they're 401(k)s or other retirement accounts, you'll likely go through your husband's employer first, but then speak directly with the firm listed on the statement. If they're other types of accounts like mutual funds or brokerage accounts, then how they're titled will determine the next steps.

2. Handle the will. If your husband had financial accounts other than retirement accounts or property in his own name, you'll have to go through the probate process with guidance from an estate attorney. However, if those assets are less than $100,000 and the spouse is the sole heir, it's possible to settle the estate with a simple form. Check with your state's register of wills office or an estate attorney.

3. Apply for life insurance benefits. Contact the insurance company that holds the policy, and they'll mail you claims forms to return with the death certificate.

4. Manage the proceeds from a life insurance policy. Take your time before you commit to any major financial decision. Working with a financial advisor who can see your overall financial picture and evaluate priorities will help you feel more in control than if you make decisions based on your current emotions.

5. Retitle accounts. As with divorce, this is an important step, especially when it comes to your home. However, I suggest that you consult with an estate attorney before doing so in case it makes sense to have a revocable living trust.

6. Apply for survivor benefits. In addition to a one-time modest Social Security death benefit, you are eligible to receive ongoing Social Security widow's benefits after age 60 based on the earnings record of your deceased spouse. However, if you are a young working spouse with children, the Social Security benefits are more complex, so please consult with a financial advisor who is knowledgeable about these benefits before making the one-time permanent election. Regrettably, the hardworking staff at the Social Security Administration are only allowed to provide you with your options. They are not allowed to give you advice and certainly cannot take into account other factors such as your ability to work and other assets you may have inherited.

Slightly lower-priority to-dos:

7. Review loans, bills, and your overall finances. After the initial must-do priorities, take time to review everything in your financial life, because your life is going to be different now in a variety of ways.

8. Cancel memberships. Review and cancel any memberships and subscriptions that you don't want.

Bigger moves, longer time frame:

9. Revisit your financial plan. Work with your financial advisor to reassess everything in your financial life. This includes your budget, savings routines, investment portfolio, financial plan, and estate plan. Make any adjustments that make sense.

10. Take your time. Recognize that if something isn't a pressing priority, it's fine to let it sit for a few weeks or longer. Don't feel any immediate pressure to get everything done ASAP. But also know that you might feel a weight off of your shoulders once you take care of everything.

11. Rely on your trusted advisors. This is the time when you'll appreciate the value of having good legal and financial professionals—your financial advisor, attorney, and accountant—who know you and can help you move forward on the right path.

12. *Get and stay organized.* Think and act in terms of simplicity. Have as few accounts as possible. Streamline bill paying and investing wherever possible by using automated payments or withdrawals.

The average age when widowhood occurs is 59. And the average 59-year-old American woman can expect to live another 25.5 more years, according to the Social Security Administration.[14]

So take your time, embrace your future, and give yourself time to adjust and enjoy the rest of your life.

I think the key takeaway should be that in the case of either divorce or death, the woman needs to know where she and her spouse stand financially. It's a middle-class millionaire woman's responsibility to know how much, where, and how the financial assets are invested. You should know your financial goals and objectives as well as the strategies being employed to reach those goals. Knowing this information will allow you to much more easily manage the transitions related to divorce or becoming a widow.

---

[14] https://www.ssa.gov/oact/STATS/table4c6.html

CHAPTER 11

Single Women Must Take Charge: Be Your Own Safety Net

We've looked at the impact of a sudden change throwing a married woman off course financially. What about the challenge of being a single woman? Someone who has never benefited from the additional household income of a partner or spouse? Someone who has no one else to fall back on but herself, for better or worse, for richer or poorer?

Consider the image of a woman climbing a mountain, starting farther down the mountain than a male associate, and doing it in high heels. With women earning less than men and living longer, there is no level playing field, not today and likely not anytime soon. Clearly, single women face a number of unique challenges. But they are not insurmountable.

Also, there are inherent or built-in financial inefficiencies in being single rather than in a dual-income household. Single men face this as well. It's simply more costly per person if you are single and living alone. For example, a single person would pay the same rent or mortgage and property tax as a married couple living in an identical place. It's estimated that in order to sustain the same lifestyle, the budget for a single person would be roughly 70 percent of that of a married couple.

Now let's look at the salary differential. Women on average reportedly earn 80 cents for every dollar that men earn. Think about how that additional 20 cents that men earn, which is actually 25 percent more than what women earn (if you do the math, $1.00 is 25 percent more than 80 cents), represents a big chunk of discretionary income. This is precisely the portion of income that can be used for retirement savings or any kind of savings, because it's beyond what you need in order to get by today or this month.

The other downside to having lower earnings is that you'll contribute less to Social Security and have lower benefits. When you compare an average single male with a single female, you can see some inherent additional financial challenges for the average single woman.

Did I mention that women typically live five or so years longer? And those years, at the tail end of one's life, just might be spent in need of expensive care, in a nursing home or with the care of a home health aide.

I think I've made my point, and my apologies if I have thoroughly depressed you. The point is clear: single women, more than any other segment of society, truly have to buckle down and do everything they can to be as financially secure as possible while having to contend with the challenge of not being fairly compensated. As a business owner and father of three hardworking, talented daughters, I cannot tell you enough how much it irks me to think they may be treated differently than their male colleagues.

On the other hand, there is a demand for women in the STEM fields—science, technology, engineering, and math—which in today's market can be used to one's advantage. For example, one of my daughters is an engineer, and doors have been opened because she is a talented female in a predominantly male industry.

My colleague Carol Petrov is another great example of someone who uses her caring demeanor to her advantage in a historically male-dominated industry. She adds a valuable complementary skill set to what I offer, including greater sensitivity to women's situations and a deeper understanding of the concerns of our female clients. It's not that I can't connect with and serve the needs of female clients, but Carol does it better and more easily, and that helps Kendall Capital to better serve our clients' needs.

Let's get down to the to-do list! Here are some things that single women can do to improve their financial well-being:

1. Be independent. As someone said in an article I recently read, "I am my own safety net." Just saying that or owning it is important. Recognizing that you need to be self-sufficient can be empowering.

2. Be diligent. That means start to save early on! Diligence begins with saving for the future at an early age. Because of the power of compounding, there's no time to lose. Those early savings, as we pointed out earlier, can be a powerful ally, as time allows them to grow more and more.

3. Be studious. The more you know about money, budgeting, planning, investing, insurance, all those personal financial topics, the better off you will be for your entire life. Go back to the first point, "Be independent; I am my own safety net." It's great to be able to lean on a trusted expert, but you'll still be better off knowing about finances and investing yourself. As they say, "Knowledge is power." In practical terms, having a decent understanding of what you are being advised to do will make it easier and clearer when following that advice. Then share what you know and inspire your friends to do the same.

4. Save more and invest aggressively. Every bit makes a difference. If you save just 1 percent more of your salary every year, it will add up. Ideally, you should save at least 10 percent of your salary, but that might be hard to do in some circumstances. Let's say you begin by saving 5 percent of your salary in a workplace retirement savings plan if that's all you can afford at first. Then see if you can bump that up to 6 percent the next year and then 7 percent the year after that and so on… That incremental increase will add up.

Similarly, for long-term investments (a time horizon of 10 years or longer), invest in a diversified mix that's primarily stocks. Don't let the terms "aggressive" or "moderately aggressive" put you off. Just understand that being 80–100 percent invested in a diversified mix of U.S. and international stocks does come with risk, but the long-term time horizon reduces that risk. There are no guarantees here, just decades and decades of real-life examples of long-term success stories that result from investing appropriately for the long term. By having a sufficiently large cash reserve account, you can afford to be more aggressive with your longer-term investments.

5. Stay healthy. A healthy lifestyle, with exercise, good nutrition, and a fulfilling social life, will help to keep you in the workforce longer (if you want to stay), and it will likely lower your health-care costs. Being single offers you the flexibility to choose a career that you want and you can just as easily change careers or locations if you find yourself in an unhealthy situation. So, much like the saying goes to "pay yourself first" when you save for retirement, strive to put yourself first when it comes to your physical and mental well-being.

6. Protect yourself. This is part of being self-sufficient and being your own safety net. In practical terms, this could involve buying disability insurance to protect against the chance that you might not be able to work at some point. After all, one in four 20 year olds will become disabled before age 67, according to the Social Security Administration.[15] So either save enough to carry you through some extended out-of-work period or buy insurance to cover a possible disability, especially if you're a homeowner and would have to remain in your home while you recovered. Medical expenses and disability are the leading cause of foreclosures.

If your employer doesn't offer disability insurance coverage as a benefit, have a professional help you determine your need to protect your income. Similarly, make sure that you address risk through adequate and appropriate life insurance and long-term care insurance.

---

[15] https://www.ssa.gov/news/press/factsheets/basicfact-alt.pdf

7. Plan thoroughly for retirement. Retirement planning involves envisioning the life and lifestyle you want; actually writing a retirement plan, which you can always revise; periodically crunching numbers and projecting or tracking progress toward your goal; and when you get close enough to retirement, such as about five years away, doing a detailed retirement budget involving projections of expenses and estimates of various sources of income.

As part of that retirement income planning, I strongly recommend waiting as long as you can before collecting Social Security benefits. That's because for every year that you wait beyond your normal retirement age—currently 66 years, but gradually rising to 67 in the next few years—before beginning to take your Social Security benefits, you'll receive 8 percent more each month for the rest of your life. If you have a family history of longevity—for example, numerous aunts or uncles or your grandparents or parents who have lived into their 90s—and you have good health habits, you definitely should prepare and plan for your savings to last well into your 90s or beyond.

Now that you are prepared to do all you can to create a lifelong marathon of independent financial security, even if it entails some sacrifices, look on the bright side. If you are a single female, you won't always be cleaning up after your spouse, nagging him to put the toilet seat down, or arguing about where to go on vacation. And you won't be tiptoeing around a challenging mother-in-law, or having to live up to her impossibly high expectations!

In fact, when you have the freedom to make your own financial decisions, embrace it. If you want to own your own home, then set about saving for that down payment, and go for it! There's no harm in building equity, and just as with other investments, the longer you're invested, the better off you'll be. Plus there is great peace of mind that comes with owning your own home. It can become a rental one day or even your retirement nest egg.

Then again, if you don't feel like being a homeowner, then turbocharge your savings while you are well employed in case a time comes when you want to make a move, get another degree, or take a phenomenal trip across Europe. My point is that single women should feel empowered to take care of themselves, enjoy their wealth, and be thankful that it's not 1960, when you needed a man to cosign your mortgage.

CHAPTER 12
Caregivers and the Sandwich Generation

We're 10 years into the wave of baby boomers retiring, and we're already seeing the impact of seniors needing long-term care. Members of the Greatest Generation, those now in their mid-80s and living beyond 100, often have pensions and equity from their homes and hold the greatest wealth in our country as an age group. For 20–30 years, they've been retired, and from their experience in the Great Depression, they know how to squeeze their pennies. They're staying in nursing homes and assisted living facilities and using home health aide services. Fortunately, they have the money to pay for their care. For what it's worth, though, 65 percent of all nursing home residents are on Medicaid, according to the AARP.

While the Greatest Generation is living longer than anticipated, the baby boomers are hot on their heels, often competing for the same caregiving resources. We knew this wave was coming, but are we prepared for the "silver tsunami" of demands for professional caregivers and facilities?

The statistics paint a pretty sobering picture of a need that will grow in the coming years. These statistics are from an article in *The New York Times*, published in December 2019, entitled "We're Getting Old, But We're Not Doing Anything About It"[16]:

- The population of the "prime caregiving age group," from 45 to 64, is expected to barely increase by 2030, while the 80-plus population is projected to grow by 79 percent, according to the *Journal of the American Medical Association*.

- An article in the *Journal of the American Geriatrics Society* forecasts that one out of seven 65 year olds today can expect to be disabled for at least five years before death.

- The risk of developing Alzheimer's disease is 14 times higher among people older than 85 than for those in the 65–69 age group.

- Eighty-three percent of help received by the elderly in the United States is provided by family members, friends, or other unpaid caregivers. Roughly two in three caregivers are women, and one-third of those aiding people with dementia are daughters.

I know that's a lot to absorb. If you're in that 45–64 age group and you're working full time to further your career, save for your retirement, and pay for college for your kids, you are not alone. You're part of the sandwich generation. You're in the

---

[16]   https://www.nytimes.com/2019/12/23/opinion/america-aging.html

middle of two demographic groups that place major demands of time and money on you and your ability to provide. So that juggling that we talked about in Chapter 8 just became even more challenging. We understand and see it often among our clients. We try to help them plan by having conversations with their parents long before there's an urgent need for their care. Ideally, their parents should have the financial resources and/ or some long-term care insurance so that it's just a matter of knowing your options and discussing them with your family. But what does it mean to be a part-time or full-time caregiver to your mother or father?

Being a caregiver can be highly stressful in a number of ways. It can affect you emotionally, physically, socially, and financially. And taking on caregiving duties for a friend or family member is much more common than you might realize. According to the AARP, an estimated 43.5 million U.S. adults have provided unpaid care to an adult or child in the past year. Six in ten of those caregivers are women. The vast majority are caring for a relative, and roughly half are caring for a parent or parent-in-law. One in 10 is providing care for a spouse.[17] They might be like one of our clients, Francine, who not only faces the reality of caring for her older husband, but she's not yet old enough for Medicare, so she must work, at least part time, in order to have health insurance benefits.

We know another couple who worked for Montgomery County, Maryland, and have retired with pensions and health insurance benefits. They've worked hard and saved for their

---

[17]   https://www.aarp.org/content/dam/aarp/ppi/2015/caregiving-in-the-united-states-2015-report-revised.pdf

retirement, and now they get to enjoy quality time with their grandchildren. In fact, it's Grandpa's "job" to meet the kids at the bus stop after school every day and to make sure their homework gets done and they have a snack. Grandpa is the "aftercare" program. Meanwhile, Grandma continues to work part time so she can earn extra money to support her 92-year-old mother, who lives in her own condominium but has in-home care. Unfortunately, Great-Grandma has dementia, but she is otherwise healthy, and it's much more affordable to have her stay in her condominium and hire the help she needs than to move to a memory-care facility. Here, the sandwich generation is like a Big Mac with an extra layer, because this retired couple is the lifeline for the older generation and two younger generations. Meanwhile, the 92-year-old matriarch has two sons in the area who could pitch in but don't, either because they wouldn't know how to or financially can't afford to. That's a shame, because they should be helping to take care of their mother, even if it's just to stop by to keep her company three evenings a week.

It seems to be commonly assumed in most families that the daughter will stop her career, even in her prime earning years (40s to late 50s), to take care of aging parents. While I greatly admire their unconditional love for their parents, too many times I don't see the loving daughter being fairly compensated by her siblings for the financial sacrifice she is assuming either by taking on a reduced work schedule or stopping work completely. As a family, they should recognize that there is not only an emotional toll placed on the daughter but also a financial toll in terms of loss of household income and savings for future goals. While it may be the best option for the family, if there are savings set aside for paying a professional caregiver, as a family they should agree that the nonprofessional caregiver deserves some compensation as well. Of course, much depends on the resources available, but it reminds me of a family we know.

The father was in his late 80s and needed home health care. Because the cost of the care was greater than the daughter, Sarah's, salary at a full-time job, the family—including Sarah's sister and two brothers—decided that it made sense for Sarah to quit her job and instead to be paid a fair market wage as a home health care worker to care for their father.

When the father died after 18 months, the family agreed to pay Sarah for an additional two months, giving her some time to find another job. Some family members thought that was very generous, while others thought it was unfair to Sarah, as it was hard for her to find another job in her mid-50s after having left the workforce for a while.

The details aren't that important, but this family's situation is a pretty typical scenario: most of the time, daughters, not sons, will take care of their parents. These women often have to change jobs, stop working or work far fewer hours, give up career advancement opportunities, and then find their way back into a suitable job after the work interruption. So it's vitally important that everyone understand the full cost and burden that women bear in taking care of elderly parents.

Additionally, if the caregiver is providing financial resources of her own, like the grandma in the previous story, if there is an inheritance, I hope the family agrees that she should be repaid before the inheritance is distributed. While this issue might not have made it into the will, it would go a long way to preserve good family relationships if the siblings recognized their father wouldn't have been able to age in his home without Sarah's extra financial support and generosity. So I believe they should compensate her properly for that when they sell their father's condominium. I think it is only fair for the daughter to be compensated for sharing her time and talent if the family has the financial resources. In my mind, it might not be based upon the hourly rate a health-care worker assumes but should be based upon that woman's fair market value of her skills and talents. I say this because too often bright, smart, talented, loving women put their careers on hold to take care of aging parents, don't accept compensation, and give up a great-paying job with excellent career potential. They receive only their portion of the parent's estate along with their siblings, who were able to continue in their respective careers. Granted, I understand and appreciate that the opportunity to devote yourself to your parents is priceless, but the caregiving woman and her siblings need to understand and appreciate the price paid for this devotion.

There are other trends we see as ways for the sandwich generation to successfully take care of their families, such as building an addition to their home and integrating their parents or in-laws long before their health declines. This idea is a good one if there's a suitable house with land, and by pooling their resources, the two generations ideally can achieve their mutual goals. This arrangement can allow for a smoother transition for all parties and is especially good motivation for the senior to start parting with furniture and personal items that can take years to whittle down! This strategy also encourages other siblings to pitch in by helping to get rid of the stuff no one wants, maybe do some home improvements, and be involved, sharing the burden of downsizing from the family home.

There are so many ways that your life could be altered by the need to provide care for a close relative. As a caregiver, you might cut back on your work hours, use some or all of your vacation time, take a leave of absence from work, or leave your job permanently to provide care to a loved one. In a 2018 survey by the Associated Press–NORC Center for Public Affairs Research, one in four caregivers said they had to cut back on their retirement savings. Four in 10 have dipped into their personal savings in order to make up for the loss of income.

Caregivers also have to give up social time and activities with friends and family because of their new role. Although many people shrug that off because of their devotion to their loved one, it does take a toll over time. The same survey found that two in five respondents said they have some type of physical or mental health condition that affects their daily lives. One in five caregivers who responded to the AARP survey said they had a high level of physical strain from caregiving, and about as many reported experiencing financial strain.

But even if you are in a good financial position, perhaps even able to retire comfortably, you may be missing out on fulfilling opportunities if you take on the role of the primary caregiver. Another difficult aspect about this role is that you don't know when it will end. So, after a few years of dedicating yourself to your aging parent, you and the family should reassess the options. This is especially true in the case of dementia, when your loved one might live for 10 years and not know the people around them. That takes a huge toll on the caregivers, be they spouses or children. They watch their quality of life screech to a halt while their loved one, who hopefully has some quality of life, is blissfully ignorant. These caregivers are especially in need of support and advocates to help them preserve as much of their own life as possible.

With all that in mind, it's vitally important to prepare for the likelihood that you could be called upon to be a caregiver one day if you haven't already. Here are some ways to shore up your finances:

Start saving early for your retirement, and invest for growth for long-term savings goals such as retirement, for better potential long-term returns. If you become a caregiver and earn less money for a while and have to pause your savings, at least your existing retirement savings can keep working for you, compounding even if you temporarily stop contributing additional money.

Save aggressively. By this I mean save as much as you can afford to stash away. Take full advantage of a matching contribution in your workplace retirement plan if your employer offers one, and add to a Roth IRA if you're eligible to do so.

Build an emergency fund to cover needs or situations like this. By building enough savings to pay for six or 12 months' worth of living expenses, you can ease your financial and emotional strain if you ever have to cut back on work hours to provide care for a family member, even part time.

Follow the frugal formula for a middle-class millionaire, which includes living within your means and avoiding high levels of debt or high-interest-rate debt. That clean personal balance sheet will be vitally important if you need to cope with a loss of income as a result of becoming a caregiver.

Accept spousal retirement contributions. If you're married and your spouse can afford it, see if you're eligible to contribute to a tax-deductible or Roth IRA as spousal contributions. The IRS allows for the nonworking spouse to make contributions so they don't fall behind on their retirement savings.

Because we are fiduciaries, we often discuss our clients' concerns that fall outside of the purview of their finances. We strive to help them address these challenges by introducing them to other professionals and reputable organizations to ease their stress and save them time. So here are some reminders that fall outside of the strict financial focus of much of this book:

- Despite the pull on your time and energy, try to make some time for yourself each week. Even a walk in nature or an exercise session at the local gym could replenish your energy and sense of balance. And that will allow you to bring more of yourself to those you love.

- Design a schedule that allows you to maintain some kind of life balance so that you avoid burnout. Even if you're financially stable, you might miss the social aspects that you had at work or the ritual of getting your favorite lunch at the diner on Mondays. Try to figure out a way for you to maintain some of the time for yourself.

There are many options, such as adult day care, where you can drop off your family member for the day and they will not only be in good hands, but it can be more social for them than staying home all day every day. There are also many professional caregiving services that offer as little as two-hour but certainly four-hour shifts so you can have a caregiver come to your home while you shop for groceries or enjoy lunch with a friend. The key is to have a regular routine that takes care of your elderly family member and can even provide them with some much-needed emotional and mental stimulation so they can enjoy their golden years. But it's also about support for the family around them, because they don't want to feel like a burden. Being able to keep going emotionally, physically, mentally, socially, and financially will help everyone in the long run.

- Advocate for yourself, and ask for help. If there are other family members, strive to find ways for them to pitch in, not only to give you a break but to help them be involved in their parent's last years or months. They may be feeling frustrated themselves and want to help but not know how. If you are alone, though, remember there are many organizations and professionals who can find you the help you need. Caring for an elderly parent is at times like caring for a child. There's no manual for it, and though your heart is in the right place, learning some techniques and giving yourself breaks will make the experience easier and more enjoyable for everyone.

CHAPTER 13

Married but Not Fully Engaged in Family Finances

I f you're married but not taking an active or fully equal role in your family's finances, including financial planning and investing, you could be putting yourself at risk. And you're not alone. A UBS Asset Management study found that 58 percent of women worldwide defer long-term financial decisions to their spouses or partners.[18]

NINE IN TEN WOMEN WILL BE ON THEIR OWN FINANCIALLY

Here's the problem, though: at least 90 percent of women will be solely responsible for their personal finances at some point in their lives largely because of divorce or widowhood. I say "at least" because in doing research for this book, we came

---

[18]   https://www.ubs.com/global/en/media/display-page-ndp//en-20190306-financial-security.html

across one study, by the Gender Gap in Financial Literacy, which used the 90 percent figure. But Wi$eUp, a financial education program for Generation X and Y women, cited a higher percentage: 99 percent. Either way, the vast majority of women will find themselves on their own one day, and they need to be prepared.

Before exploring how to become more involved in your personal finances, let's look at how and why many women are so financially unengaged.

While society has made a lot of progress toward gender equality, we still largely fall into social stereotypes. Males are often encouraged to follow math and science, and females are less so. I hesitate to speculate that men are more inclined to be nerdy number crunchers, but there are studies and insights that point to that tendency.

While a stereotypical guy might delve into the minutiae of competitive annual stock market returns, just as he might have memorized batting averages and other baseball statistics at age 13, a woman is more likely to focus on qualitative issues. She might just want to know, "Am I at risk of outliving my money? Will I be able to maintain my lifestyle in retirement?"

Now let's look at a typical family situation. The married couple, Jim and Janet, realize they should both be somewhat involved in the family finances, but they don't want to duplicate each other's efforts. Because Jim is more interested in and comfortable with investing, he takes care of that. Meanwhile, Janet does more of their day-to-day shopping for groceries and other household items, and she's more involved in their children's needs and activities. So naturally she'll focus on those shorter-term or more immediate concerns.

In an ideal world, Jim and Janet would share the information and consult with one another. Unfortunately, that doesn't happen very much. Janet just isn't interested in investments, and she finds it pretty confusing. She has as much interest in investment ROIs and IRAs as she did in baseball RBIs and ERAs a few decades ago, which is to say none! So there's a knowledge gap that never gets addressed.

On a more serious note, sometimes it's not just a knowledge gap but also a wealth and power gap that develops. If the man earns more money, he might feel he should have more say in financial matters. Taking this to an unhealthy level, some men can be controlling, and I've read and heard some horror stories of an uninformed woman in a marriage having no idea about the millions of dollars they had as a couple while she lived on a meager allowance. And sometimes, without any malevolence, a couple might just get into a situation where the wife is uninformed and unprepared to make big financial decisions until forced to because of divorce or the death of her spouse.

Now that we've established why a lot of women are taking a back seat to their husbands on family finances, let's see how you could change this for the better.

Communicate. It's easy to get caught up in the endless tasks of running a household, and we all lead busy lives, but make time to talk with your spouse about money. This could include casual chats about things that might seem innocuous but could be quite telling. For instance, I read about a married couple that had sharply different views about whether they should pay for their children's college or teach them independence by not doing so. That's fine. But the couple had been married a decade before that conversation suddenly came up and precipitated a lot of marital tension.

Monthly check-ins. Let's assume that one spouse handles the shorter-term monthly household budgeting and the other takes care of long-term investments, retirement planning, life insurance, and the like. That's fine, but why not plan a monthly family finances summit? That's where you will have a regular opportunity to share and discuss anything important. Of course, it needn't be so formal. Any regular chat about finances in which the less-involved partner is consulted could go a long way toward a healthier relationship and a better-prepared partner down the road.

Both meet with your financial advisor. We have plenty of clients whom we see as couples, and with many others, we will typically only see the husband. When asked why his wife isn't with him, Mr. Smith will typically say, "Well, she just isn't interested, and anyway, she trusts my judgment." That's shortsighted thinking for all of the reasons mentioned above.

Instead of entirely deferring, accompany your spouse to a meeting with your financial advisor once a year or even every other year. Ask questions if you don't understand something. Weigh in. Get involved. This is your money too. This is your financial future. As a financial advisor, I'd much rather be working with a widow or recently divorced female client who already knows the basics than to have to teach her personal finance 101 while she is going through an emotionally challenging time.

Strategize together on Social Security benefits. Here's a different reason why it pays to both be involved. Deciding when and how to take your Social Security benefits can lead to higher overall lifetime benefits when acting as a couple. Often it's in the best interests of the couple for the higher-income earner to defer benefits to age 70. That's because the benefit grows by 8 percent per year of deferral past the "full retirement age," which is now between 66 and 67. Often it's the man who earned a higher salary and worked more years, which naturally generates a higher benefit. So, while his benefit is delayed, the couple can take the wife's benefit to take advantage of some retirement income. Then, since he is statistically likely to die before his wife, she as a widow will be able to receive his higher benefits for life.

These are general tendencies, and there are plenty of exceptions, but just to illustrate the benefits of a coordinated approach, you can see the value of working together on this. That begins with the two of you being aware, knowledgeable about, and involved with your family finances.

What you should know. No matter how involved or uninvolved you are financially, at least know the following points:

- What you earned last year as a couple. Just look over the final tax return, even if your tax preparer signed it.

- Your combined net worth—all that you own minus all that you owe. You should also have a basic understanding of the types of assets you own so that you know what's liquid or might not be as easy to access.

- What your will says. Is it up to date? Are all your beneficiaries up to date on all your retirement investment accounts and insurance policies?

- Where all of your important financial documents are located, along with account-holder names and passwords for online access.

A little shared knowledge and communication about money can go a very long way. As a couple, you can also be role models for your children. It's no different than making sure Dad knows how to feed the baby and change its diapers in case Mom isn't around to do so. Or that Mom knows how to mow the lawn and start a fire in the fireplace if Dad isn't around. Knowledge is powerful and brings with it great confidence and understanding of each other's familiar roles. Just because you choose roles out of convenience or accentuating one's talents doesn't mean your partner should completely abdicate knowledge of those duties.

If you're not already involved in your family finances, start now. You won't regret it. Want proof? In the UBS study, 98 percent of divorced and widowed women said they encouraged others to be more involved.

SECTION IV

Life Stages

In this section of *Middle-Class Millionaire Women*, we take another perspective on the financial challenges and opportunities you'll face throughout your lifetime. Females of all ages, from young childhood to the late stages of life, can benefit greatly from adopting healthy lifelong financial habits and the middle-class millionaire mentality.

In the next chapter, "How to Raise Financially Savvy Kids," we look at the ways that you can teach children of both genders important real-life money lessons at an early age, but we show how this can be especially important for girls.

CHAPTER 14

How to Raise Financially Savvy Kids

W e have a financial literacy problem in this country. This is evident by the fact that the United States ranked 14th in the world, with only 57 percent of adults considered financially literate, according to the Standard & Poor's Ratings Services Global Financial Literacy Survey.[19] While many other countries make financial literacy part of their curriculum, our philosophy is to leave it up to the states to decide if classroom time should be devoted to the topic. Meanwhile, the onus is on parents or other adults, such as Boy Scout troop leaders, to teach our children about money. But what if your parents weren't financially savvy themselves? What if they had pensions and didn't have 401(k)s or Roth IRAs? What if you had to learn the hard way?

Clearly, you're keen to break that cycle, because you're reading this book. So here are some lessons that can be woven into everyday living from an early age. It's important to recognize,

---

[19] https://www.investopedia.com/the-push-to-make-financial-literacy-into-law-4628372

too, that women have not always had the opportunities to manage their own wealth or to even learn how to do it. Thankfully, that's in the past, and as we look to our children's future, not only can girls learn from a mom or grandma who worked and managed her own wealth, but several of our states have recognized that it's important to teach some basics to all children at various ages.

Across the nation, though, only 17 states require high school students to take a course in personal finance, and only five states do it well, according to a report by the Champlain College Center for Financial Literacy. A few other states, such as New Jersey, are beginning to teach middle schoolers. Here in Montgomery County, Maryland, we are fortunate to have a program called Finance Park through Junior Achievement of Greater Washington, which put together a three-week curriculum for seventh graders in a partnership with our schools and businesses. So let's work together to bring up our financial literacy rates starting now!

This chapter is broken into four sections. The first three, which apply to both boys and girls, give practical tips for things you can do for or with your kids at three key stages—preschool, school age, and preteen/teenage years. The final section is focused entirely on girls.

HOW TO TEACH YOUNGER CHILDREN ABOUT MONEY

Show them that coins have value. You can introduce young children to money by letting them play with a toy set of plastic coins and a cash register. By playing store with young kids, you can introduce them to the idea of purchasing things and that it's not just by clicking a button on your phone.

MONEY LESSONS FOR SCHOOL-AGE KIDS

As children enter school, they'll be able to grasp more. So you can gradually introduce more complex concepts and use hands-on opportunities to introduce them to financially responsible behavior.

Take them grocery shopping as a field trip. We don't tend to think of things like weekly grocery shopping as a field trip, but if you're focused on the learning that could happen, you could set in motion a lifetime of financial responsibility. At the same time, you could possibly transform a bored and restless young child into one who is actively learning to comparison shop. Talk to your children about the prices of certain items and their packaging so they learn about unit prices. As they get older, talk about bulk discounts and sales to learn whether something is really a good deal or not.

Have ongoing casual money conversations. As children mature and are ready to absorb more, you can gradually get into more advanced everyday discussions about money. When you think about it, money affects our lives in endless ways. There are countless opportunities to teach your kids in a casual everyday sense using items they're interested in, such as clothing, toys, and candy. Explain impulse purchases and why stores place certain items near the cash register. Suggest spending less money on one item in order to save a little more for something special. Discuss gas efficiency and trade-offs on what car you drive or might purchase. Look for daily opportunities to teach and inspire the next generation of middle-class millionaires. While you're at it, these moments are also good times to compare material things with experiences and why you might make do with the same sneakers a little longer so you can spend some money at the local bounce house this weekend.

Use a clear jar to show savings. Even though we use less and less cash, young children will understand physical coins and cash much more easily than the more abstract idea of credit and debit cards and electronic payment. Rather than use a piggy bank, place money for them in a clear jar. And consider three jars: one each for spending, saving for delayed gratification, and charitable giving.

Share about sharing. You can teach young children about the value of generosity and how good it feels when you do something nice for someone else. This can start at a basic level even before they enter school.

Needs versus wants; now versus wait. The money management lesson associated with an allowance, which can apply to any money your children receive or earn, is that ultimately they can choose to spend now or save for later, and that delayed gratification could pay off in wonderful ways. Consider the trade-off, for example, between frequent candy purchases, which are gone almost immediately, or saving up for a toy like a stuffed animal or the latest action figure, which they can play with for a long time. Having ongoing chats about whether something is a need or a want is one of the most important money lessons.

Open a bank account. Studies have shown that children who had a bank account scored higher on financial literacy measures than those who didn't have a bank account. Being able to see their balances grow over time can encourage children to save more. Help them read and understand their bank statement, and talk about ways to save and what they might want to save up for.

Give them incentives to save. You can encourage your children to save their allowance and other income in the same way that employers/401(k) savings plan sponsors encourage their employees to save: match their savings. You could match contributions to their savings accounts dollar for dollar each month or provide a year-end matching bonus for the amount that their bank balance has grown over the year. If they save $200 and you match that, they'll have $400.

Let them make mistakes. In trying to teach children financial responsibility, you might be inclined to direct them or control their decisions. But this is their money, and it's ultimately up to them to decide what to do with it. Importantly, they will learn to make smarter choices if they sometimes don't make the best choices and then face the negative consequences. For example, if they blow through this month's allowance before they're due to receive next month's, and if you don't give them an advance, your children are more likely to remember the experience and learn from it.

Allowance: To give or not to give? In addition to money that they might receive as a birthday gift or a mysterious present from the tooth fairy, you can give your children an age-appropriate allowance. A common approach is $1 per week for their age. A six year old would receive $6 per week, and a 12-year-old would receive $12 per week. As children grow older, perhaps you could switch to a monthly allowance, teaching them the value of pacing their expenditures until the next "payday."

The big benefit to an allowance is teaching responsibility. Part of that is not bailing out your children with an advance on next week's allowance if they spend all their money too soon. Also, encourage them to save some money for later, give some to charity, and spend some on what they want now.

However, the allowance scheme doesn't work for all families. If your kid tends to spend money as soon as he gets it despite your efforts, and wants to buy something with next week's allowance, then you should probably reconsider. Also, let's face it: a lot of us don't have cash in our wallets these days, so unless you can commit to giving your child the dollar bills and fulfilling your end of the bargain, perhaps you should skip allowance and opt for a monthly subscription to their favorite game or streaming channel instead.

Give your kids the opportunity to earn more. If you do decide to give an allowance, consider giving your children the opportunity to earn extra money. Extra chores for cash could include sweeping the garage, weeding the garden, or vacuuming and washing your car. Some parents believe in only offering the opportunity to earn money for extra chores and emphasize to their children that there are set chores they're expected to do just because they are members of the family and share the home.

Preteens and teens can learn more advanced money lessons

Encourage entrepreneurs. As your children reach their early teens and even preteen years, encourage them to earn money outside of your house doing neighborhood jobs, such as babysitting, dog walking, lawn mowing, gardening, or raking. They'll enjoy earning that extra money and dreaming up ways to spend or save it.

Give them stock. You can do something similar to what I did with my four children. Every year, I would give each of them $500 worth of stock at Christmas. These shares of companies like McDonald's, Microsoft, and Verizon didn't mean much to them when they were young. But over time, as they grew up and their investments grew, they appreciated these stock gifts more and more. You can go beyond that and actively discuss and review potential stocks that you could add to your or their portfolios.

Show them how to budget. Receiving an allowance and having a bank account provides your kids an opportunity to learn about and practice budgeting. You can help them track what they receive, save, and spend each month with a simple notebook or spreadsheet. By the time they're adults, budgeting will be second nature. Have you noticed how many money management apps there are these days? Try one yourself, and have your children use it from the start. They won't know what you mean by balancing your checkbook, but they'll learn how to set an alert to text them when their bank account drops below a certain limit.

Discuss the dangers of debt. As your teenagers approach college age, they'll receive credit card offers, and as they reach driving and auto-purchasing age, they might have a car loan to deal with. This is the time for them to be fully aware of the dangers or risks of debt, especially high-interest-rate credit card debt, which can be a powerful, alluring trap. These are among the most valuable lessons you can impart to your budding adult child: Build your credit score. Don't spend what you don't have.

This can be a great time to discuss major purchases, such as a car or college tuition. We can learn from the mistakes of previous generations and see the heavy burden they bear from student loan debt. Talk with friends or family members who have been there, and have frank conversations about what you can afford as a family. If you've saved in a 529 plan, that's great! If you plan to contribute to the cost from your current income, make sure you don't do it to the detriment of your own retirement savings. Be honest and clear with your teen if you expect him or her to pitch in financially; that will help your child to apply to schools with realistic expectations.

Be a role model. How often do we hear "Do as I say, not as I do"? If that's your approach to financial management, what you say might not be worth much. Your actions as a role model do speak much louder than your words. Model the behavior that you seek in your children: Budget properly. Pay your bills on time. Don't carry a credit card balance.

But you're allowed to be imperfect, and you could even come clean with your kids and share your mistakes with them so that they—as well as you—can learn from them.

- Perhaps you spent too much at some point, didn't create an emergency fund, and paid the price with a credit card debt that took a while to pay off.

- Maybe you regret an impulse purchase of some item that you never used.

- Maybe you waited too long to begin saving earnestly for your retirement and now have to double down to catch up.

These all could be great learning experiences for the whole family if you position them in that way.

Encourage early retirement savings. As your older teenagers begin to earn money, even in a part-time job, encourage them to open a Roth individual retirement account (IRA). Even a modest $1,000 will likely grow appreciably over the next half century or longer. The sooner they begin to save for their most important financial goal, the better off they'll be.

For girls especially

Encourage your daughters to learn and apply math. "I'm no good with numbers" is not an acceptable excuse for not being involved in your personal finances, and that goes double for your daughters. Given all that you know, give your daughters every chance to apply math in comparison shopping, budgeting, and the like.

Debunk the notion of a Prince Charming. Fairy tales *can* come true, but don't hold your breath. In the real world, your daughter might be on her own financially for many or all of her adult years. As noted in earlier chapters, even a blissful marriage, in which your spouse handles all the finances, might end one day because of divorce or death. So all women need to be prepared to be their own money manager. Besides, your daughter might fall in love with a great guy who doesn't know a thing about managing money. If so, he'll be relieved to rely on her for navigating their financial future.

Teach investing and long-range financial planning. Even if you don't have a love or affinity for investing, make sure that your daughters have the opportunity to learn about investing and long-range planning at an early age. That could be enormously beneficial as they go through their adult lives.

Discuss female stereotypes versus middle-class-millionaire values. Talk about how females are portrayed in the media and advertising, and compare those messages of consumerism and material-related happiness with the middle-class-millionaire values that you adhere to. This is a great time to talk about needs versus wants in the context of image and inner beauty versus exterior looks.

Girls are targeted from a very early age to look a certain way and pay for clothes, manicures, and makeup to get that look. Whether your girl is athletic or a bookworm, at some level she wants to fit in and feel good about herself, which is normal and healthy. But just like everything else, she can learn how to use her money toward what matters most, and if a precedent is started, such as shopping for the hottest trends in the fall or having a manicure every two weeks, then she will likely see that as a need when she becomes an adult. Instead, she can learn how to wear what she needs—for example, high-quality running shoes for the athlete—but she can buy the rest of her athletic clothes from a discount store.

Discuss careers and earning opportunities. Talk with your daughters about what they love to do, what they're good at, and how they might make money at those things in a career. You're not a guidance counselor, "just" a parent, but you can begin to raise your daughters' awareness about possible careers and what they can expect to earn and prepare them for major life decisions. If they insist on new designer clothes and manicures, then they had better aim for high-paying jobs. Until they earn the big bucks, they can enjoy finding treasures at the consignment shop.

It's a long way from "What is a penny worth versus a quarter?" to "What do you want to do for the rest of your life?" Your special role as a parent, and especially a mother to your daughters, involves teaching them the life skills and values that will set them up for lifelong personal financial success. Don't ever get discouraged or downplay the enormous role you play every day as their parent and role model, and try to always have fun with it.

CHAPTER 15

Starting Out Strong for a Lifetime of Financial Success

A s you start your career as a young woman, what you do now with your finances will shape the rest of your life. If you make major financial mistakes, such as living extravagantly, not paying your bills, racking up large credit card debts, or failing to save any money, you'll risk being in a financial hole for a very long time.

This chapter has guidance to help you get ahead of the game financially and set yourself up for a lifetime of financial success. The steps to take aren't complicated, but they can be challenging because you'll need some discipline. Once you develop good financial habits, though, you'll be on the path to becoming a financially secure, empowered middle-class millionaire woman.

Steps Toward Personal Financial Success

SPEND LESS THAN YOU EARN

It's kind of simple, isn't it? If you keep spending less than you earn—in other words, living within your means—you'll be able to gradually accumulate wealth. If you have any debt, such as a student loan, you'll be able to pay it off steadily. With every paycheck, if you can be disciplined and put aside some money, you'll keep adding to your nest egg rather than depleting it. Get in this habit early on and it'll be second nature through the rest of your life. And you'll be on the road to financial security. You'll thank yourself later.

PAY YOURSELF FIRST

One way to make sure you save money each pay period or each month is to set up an automatic transfer from your checking account into a savings account or an investment account every two weeks or once a month. Another option available in many workplaces is to have part of your paycheck—for example, 10 percent of your earnings—go to a savings account separate from your checking account every payday. When you don't have the money in your hand or available in your checking account, you can't spend it. This automatic, foolproof way of saving will grow your savings over time without you having to think about it.

Look at how much money you could save over time for a goal such as a down payment for a vehicle or a house. Without counting any earnings, if you set aside $200 a month, you could have:

$2,400	…after one year
$4,800	…after two years
$7,200	…after three years
$9,600	…after four years
$12,000	…after five years

By committing to that savings every pay period and having it automatically transferred, you'll ensure steady progress toward any goal.

BUILD AN EMERGENCY FUND

Once you are able to live within your means and develop that automatic savings routine, create an emergency fund. This is money that you can set aside in a safe, conservative bank account, money market account, or certificate of deposit. These accounts won't earn much interest, but that's fine. Low returns means taking low (or no) risk, and that's important because this is money that you want to be there when you need it.

Ideally, you should have enough money available in an emergency account to be able to pay at least six months of living expenses in case you lose your job or incur unusually high bills that could be difficult to pay off. That's the rough guideline. But women whose compensation may vary, such as a commission-based salesperson or a real estate agent, should probably have more than six months' worth of emergency funds.

We had a highly successful female client who worked as a commissioned salesperson selling to the federal government. She would earn $300,000 to $500,000 per year, with a modest base salary of $50,000; the rest she received as an end-of-year bonus. She needed more than six months of emergency funds to be able to manage through the ups and downs of that irregular payment cycle. On the other side of coin, we work with several middle-class millionaire women who receive steady paychecks every two weeks from the federal, state, or local government. For these women, having six months of emergency funds would likely be plenty.

As a rule of thumb, six months of emergency funds would mean being able to cover your core monthly expenses, such as rent, car payments, insurance, utilities, and groceries, for a half year. Having that on hand could help you handle an emergency, such as a layoff during the coronavirus pandemic, without having to rack up hefty credit card bills or borrow money from the bank or a friend or relative. That's empowering!

PAY OFF YOUR DEBT

Some of us enter adulthood with substantial student debt. Depending on the amount of that debt and your earnings, it could take you years or even decades to pay it all off. One thing to keep in mind is that you can make gradual progress on multiple financial fronts. Read or revisit Chapter 8 on juggling multiple financial goals.

Don't ignore your student debt, but don't let your desire to pay it off prevent you from making progress on other key goals, like saving for your retirement. Critically important with any debt is the interest rate that you're charged. With really high-interest debt, such as credit card balances, where you might be charged 20 percent, 25 percent, or even more, pay it off ASAP.

But with more modest interest rates that might be roughly in line with what you might expect to earn on an investment—let's say 6–8 percent—it's pretty much a wash. In that case, there's less urgency to pay it off quickly, but of course, once you pay it off, you'll have a weight removed from your shoulders, and you'll have newfound financial freedom and flexibility.

While we're on the topic of debt, try and be judicious about adding new debts. Some types of debt are inevitable or hard to avoid, such as a mortgage, which could open the door to greater long-term financial security. Without getting into an analysis of the pros and cons of owning or renting your home or apartment, if you want to own your home, you'll need a mortgage loan. And you'll likely need a loan to buy a new vehicle, even if you have some money saved so as to lower your monthly loan payments. As long as you can fit those monthly car loan or mortgage payments into your budget, and the vehicle or place of residence is a necessity rather than an extravagant luxury, that's fine.

BUILD A STRONG CREDIT SCORE

Your worthiness to receive a loan from a bank or credit union is measured by your credit score. It's vitally important to build a good credit score, which is expressed as a number between 300 and 850. The higher the number the better, which means you'll be more likely to get a loan and to pay a lower interest rate because you'll be seen as a better risk for a lender. In other words, they'll have a better chance of being repaid for the loan.

It's hard to believe, but as recently as the 1960s, a woman needed a man to cosign to obtain a credit card from some card issuers. It didn't matter if she was college educated and had a full-time job, she could simply be refused the opportunity to even build a credit score. Much like the suffragists, women still recently have fought and persisted to be treated on equal footing to men when applying for credit or a mortgage on their own.

So, if you're a young woman, don't take your good credit for granted. It's now available to you when you turn 18 and will increase as long as you handle it responsibly. Simply, make sure to do these things and your credit score will be good:

- Pay all your bills in full whenever you can. And if you can't pay in full, make sure that you pay on time, even if it's just the minimum. To make sure you don't forget, you can use technology, such as autopay or online bill pay reminders. A day late is the same as a month late to creditors, so don't be late! If you are late or going to be late, make sure you call the creditors and let them know right away. They may be willing to work with you so that your credit score is not affected.

- Don't use more of your total credit card limit than you need to; it's best to keep your card balance at no more than 30 percent of that card's credit limit. If you're really in a pinch, rather than have a single card with a balance that's close to the limit, you're better off opening a second card and having two with low balances. Or you could ask the card company to raise your limit and stick with a single card.

- Don't default on any loans or declare bankruptcy.

- Don't close credit accounts that show a long, reliable history of paying your bills on time. Lenders will want to see those long-term financially responsible habits.

- Don't be tempted to open too many cards, either, especially store cards unless you use them frequently. Store cards have the highest interest rates, which makes them dangerously costly if you can't pay them in full every time. If that's the case, just say no when the cashier asks you to open a card to save 5 percent on your shopping bill. That one-time 5 percent savings will likely be far less than the interest you'll pay if you carry a balance.

- Pay other bills on time as well, including your cell phone, rent, and utility bills.

Having great credit is a key building block of financial security. It takes time to build up, so make sure you protect it. Once your credit is damaged, it may be harder for you to get ahead in life, whether it's renting an apartment in a nice neighborhood or getting the best rate on your next car loan.

Many credit card companies offer free or low-priced credit monitoring, which will alert you if someone opens a credit card in your name. They also offer ways to quickly and temporarily shut down your credit card if you lose it or have your purse stolen. Be vigilant in protecting your credit, and consider enrolling in an identity protection program that also can help you restore your good credit if your identity is stolen.

Of course, practicing one good financial habit will make it easier to develop another one. For example, if you steadily save money and pay off your debts, it will be easier to build an emergency fund, which will help to keep you out of financial trouble, and your credit score will reflect that.

SAVE FOR YOUR RETIREMENT

I know it's hard to tackle a variety of goals at once, and you'll have some pressing financial needs and priorities as you enter your earning years. But even with competing goals, it's great if you can start to save for your retirement your first week in the working world. And it's easy if your employer-sponsored retirement plan—such as a 401(k), 403(b), or 457 plan—offers automatic enrollment. No workplace plan? No problem. Save in an individual retirement account (IRA). Do this even modestly in your first year or two of earning money as an adult and you'll be getting ahead of the game.

How much money will you need to save for your retirement? It's impossible to know in your early or mid-20s. But it could easily be $1 million, $2 million, or a fair bit more depending on your lifestyle. The point is you have to rely upon yourself when you become elderly, and the more you save, the more options you'll have to live a comfortable retirement.

I know it can be hard to envision, especially if you're in your 20s, but you may know an older neighbor or family friend who is struggling to make ends meet or has to work a job they don't like when they would rather be retired. How can you avoid that situation in a few decades? What you do now will matter later.

Unfortunately, fewer and fewer employers offer traditional pension plans. And Social Security benefits were designed to cover only one-third or so of your retirement expenses. By starting to save early, you have the power of compound interest, and you might be surprised to see how quickly your accounts grow. Plus, if you start young and amass a large retirement account balance in the first 20 years of your career, you may be able to downshift your retirement savings later on as other goals, such as paying for day care or saving for college, begin to compete as financial priorities.

I just met with a couple the other day who are in their mid-40s. I was impressed with how much they had saved in their retirement accounts. They were "maxers" from the beginning, meaning they always tried to save as much as allowed in their retirement accounts. Now that they have two small children, they're feeling the squeeze of childcare costs and the need to increase their take-home pay for a few years until the children are in public school. At that point, they'll save on day care but will want to be saving for college.

As we said earlier, it's a balancing act, but getting started early will allow you the peace of mind to be able to lower your retirement savings contributions for a few years should you need to in order to meet your current goals.

Don't worry about saving an enormous sum. Just start saving early on and you won't need to save nearly as much later because your money will be growing, earning a return on its own. Try to save 15 percent of your income and increase it with each raise or promotion. You will learn to live without that amount, trust me. My advice is to try to save at least 10 percent for retirement, perhaps 5 percent for other shorter-term goals, give some regularly to charity, and enjoy life with 80 percent of your earnings. Do that over your lifetime and you will enjoy financial freedom while accumulating funds while working and during retirement.

EDUCATE YOURSELF ABOUT MONEY MANAGEMENT

Knowledge is power. And knowledge about money matters will not only empower you, it could allow you to become financially secure and confident in your decisions. Even if you're working with a great advisor whom you trust, you want to be conversant with the key financial matters that will affect your life and your key life decisions.

It doesn't take a lot to learn the basics. Books like this one will help. Reading financial publications, such as *Kiplinger's* and *Money* magazine, will also be beneficial. The *Wall Street Journal* has plenty of informative articles, and now there are various apps, such as NerdWallet and Mint, plus podcasts and even people on YouTube who share brief tidbits to add to your knowledge and help you stay on track. But try and avoid paying attention to "the noise," which is a way of describing the day-to-day nonsense that can trip up investors, who should generally be looking at long-term goals and the good consistent habits that middle-class millionaires adopt early on and follow throughout their lives.

Learn the basics of personal finance, and try and focus on timeless wisdom rather than short-term information.

SET FINANCIAL GOALS, AND TRACK YOUR PROGRESS

Setting goals is critically important. Think about what is most important to you. Set specific goals with time lines. Then develop strategies that will guide you on how and when you can expect to meet those goals. Think about so-called SMART goals: specific, measurable, achievable, realistic, and timely.

For example, *I will save $15,000 in the next three years so that I will be able to have a down payment to buy a house.* Then you can break that down into how you can achieve that goal. Without factoring in earnings on your savings, $15,000 in three years means $5,000 a year. That's roughly $400 a month. Can you save $400 a month? If not, readjust your goal to make it achievable and realistic, and perhaps extend the three years to four or five years.

To save $15,000 over five years, you'd just need to save $3,000 a year, or $250 a month. That's much easier to do. By working with concrete numbers, you'll be able to take concrete action, measure your progress, and achieve your goal.

You can apply this approach to any goals: paying off student debt, buying a car or truck, building an emergency fund, or saving for your retirement.

BE INVOLVED IN YOUR FAMILY FINANCES

If you haven't read Chapter 10 ("When Life Throws You a Curveball") or Chapter 13 ("Married but Not Fully Engaged in Family Finances"), I encourage you to do so. They discuss in great detail the risks that can befall women who are overly reliant on their spouses or partners for financial knowledge. Take the steps to know the basics of your family finances no matter what your situation, regardless of how you and your significant other have carved out financial responsibilities. It could save you much grief one day, and it should be healthy for your relationship.

GROW YOUR INCOME

Much of this chapter has been focused on financial responsibility, frugality, and good saving and spending habits. The other side of the coin, so to speak, is earning. If you are able to earn more money, you'll be in better financial shape, all other things being equal. If you are well educated, you're likely to earn more money over the course of your life, although that often is determined by the availability of jobs for someone with your education. So consider an educational path that leads to jobs that are in demand or that offer student loan reimbursement.

You may start out in a job that you don't particularly love but that offers valuable experience and benefits. Meanwhile, you could consider a side gig to add to your income and savings while feeling more fulfilled and perhaps save for the next degree, if that's your path. If not, perhaps the side gig could help you build a down payment for a car or house.

If you are able to, before you enter college and determine your degree, get an idea of the approximate salary ranges that diploma will offer when you graduate. One of my daughters went to Clemson University, initially wanting to be a graphic designer. Now, I am all for helping your children follow their dreams. I also believe it is a parent's responsibility to help daughters fully understand and envision their respective dreams.

I talked with my daughter about what a graphic designer's life would be like and what career opportunities she would have, and about the opportunities she would have as an engineer. Aside from being higher up in the corporate world, if she ever wanted to change careers, she'd find it easier to move from engineering to graphic design than the opposite. My daughter ended up majoring in industrial engineering, and so far she's had a successful career working for several Fortune 500 companies.

My point is to strive to save no matter where you are in your career. Having good credit and an emergency fund will serve you well at any stage of life. And if your goal is to be self-employed or run your own business, then there should be a correlation between how hard you work and how much you earn. Similarly, being your own boss means taking extra measures to ensure financial security.

As I'm writing this book, we're seeing the financial hardships brought on by the COVID-19 pandemic. For many small-business owners and self-employed people, it's a devastating blow to their ability to earn a living and take care of their employees. So, if your passions lead you down that path, understand that you need to have even more savings for yourself and your business to be able to weather a crisis in which you might not have any revenue for several months. I truly believe that life is a journey, and these tips will help you to be able to realize your full potential.

There you have it: 10 tips that could help you set yourself up for a life of financial success. They're not rocket science. Anyone can develop good financial habits, learn the basics about personal finance, and live the life of a middle-class millionaire. It is just a question of doing it.

CHAPTER 16
Catching Up Quickly and Effectively

For a variety of reasons, you might realize at age 40 or 50 that you are not as financially prepared as you should be for retirement. Perhaps you had some health setbacks, career missteps, or a messy and costly divorce. These things happen. But now you have a lifetime of experience, optimism, determination, and a goal to retire someday and maintain your independence as long as you can.

There's no reason to despair. Instead, take action. There are plenty of steps you can take to become better prepared for retirement or more financially secure despite a slow or delayed start. To begin, assess your finances, learn your options, calculate your needs, and commit to yourself.

Action Steps You Can Take in Your 40s or 50s That Can Go a Long Way

1. Assess where you are and where you need to be, and plan how to get there. The first step to improve your financial security is to assess where you are right now, set a realistic goal, and then create a plan to move from point A (today) to point B (your retirement savings goal).

Here are some key questions:

- How much have you saved so far in your retirement accounts and in general?

- What is your overall net worth? Tally all that you own and subtract what you owe.

- How much money do you think you'll need to save before you're financially ready to retire? If you have a pension from your employer, that's a bonus, but fewer of us have that anymore.

- When do you plan to take your Social Security benefits? Many people take them at age 62, as soon as they are able to, but that is often a major mistake, because if you can afford to delay taking your benefits, those benefits will grow by 8 percent for every year that you delay until the maximum age of 70. We'll talk about Social Security benefits strategies in greater depth in the next chapter, "Going the Distance." But having a rough idea of when you'll take those benefits will help you plan ahead of time.

2. Put together a tentative retirement budget. To figure out a realistic savings goal, begin by making a tentative retirement budget. This is much more beneficial than just relying on a quick rule of thumb such as "plan to spend 80 percent (or any other arbitrary number) of your current income in retirement." We're all different, and there are so many important factors to consider, such as: Will your mortgage be paid off? Do you expect to downsize into smaller and less expensive housing? How much do you expect to travel? Will your health insurance be covered as a retirement benefit? Are you in good health?

Begin by looking at your current expenses, and then try to project (even roughly) what your expenses might look like in retirement. If you're still 15 or 20 years from retirement, this could involve a lot of guesswork. But it'll be helpful to have even a rough target to aim for. A lot of people who don't do this exercise really have very little sense of how much they need to have saved before they leave work.

If you're within five years of retirement, you'll be working with more accurate and precise numbers that could really give you a good sense of what your finances will be like in retirement and when you'll be financially secure enough to retire.

Some expense items, such as your mortgage, might no longer exist. If you downsize from a large house to a smaller condo or apartment, you might save on a variety of regular, fixed expenses, including property tax, insurance, and utility bills, along with any mortgage payments. So tally up your annual housing costs, including mortgage, insurance, property tax, and utilities. Think of these separately from expenses that stay pretty much the same wherever you live, such as groceries or your cell phone, and take into account ongoing discretionary spending—things that will appear on your monthly credit card bill—as well as debts such as a car loan if you tend to buy a new car every few years.

Think about the cost of health insurance. Buying your own health insurance in your early 60s could cost $400–$700 per month. Once you turn 65, you can and should apply for Medicare B. In addition to your basic Medicare coverage, you will likely want a Medicare supplement plan, which typically costs $200–$400 per month depending on your desired coverage. Also, have an idea of how you'll handle long-term care costs. You could buy long-term care insurance or consider self-insuring, which means saving dedicated money aside from your retirement savings so that you can pay for any help that you might need late in life, whether in your own home or a facility.

We discuss both health-care and long-term care costs and options in greater detail in the next chapter. For now, factor in some kind of guesstimate on costs so that you can budget realistically. Some good resources include the AARP and the annual Genworth report that breaks down the costs of a variety of care situations in all 50 states. See Chapter 17 for more detail on that.

And of course, factor in some fun or discretionary expenses. You'll have a lot more time on your hands once you're no longer working. Retirement is about being able to enjoy yourself. Think about the things you enjoy and what that'll cost, and include money in your annual budget for the fun stuff. This might motivate you to save more or to consider working part time in retirement so that you earn some "play money."

Also recognize, without getting too much into the weeds, that through your early retirement years, you might see some expenses rise initially, including travel and leisure activities, such as golf and more frequent dinners out. Over time, however, these might decline as you settle into a less active pace. Eventually, perhaps in your 80s and 90s, you might spend very little on leisure activities and a lot more on health-care costs.

Once you have your monthly or annual retirement expenses estimated, tally your anticipated income, including Social Security benefits and any pension benefits. The difference between your estimated expenses and these income totals is the amount that you'll have to fund from your retirement savings. You also might factor in income from a future part-time job in retirement if you see yourself still working.

There are a number of good websites with retirement savings and budgeting calculators, such as this one from the AARP: https://www.aarp.org/work/retirement-planning/retirement_calculator.html.

3. Consider working with a CERTIFIED FINANCIAL PLANNER™ professional. Even working with a good, thorough, well-designed retirement calculator can raise as many questions as it answers:

- What is a realistic rate of return?

- What are the risks of having expectations that are too high?

- What if you lose your job or are not physically able to work any longer?

- What are the chances that you will be able to work beyond retirement age, should you be in financial need?

- What other investment strategies could improve your investment earnings without exposing you to undue risk?

A good financial planner can work with you to answer these questions in a way that respects and reflects who you are individually as a saver, investor, and consumer. Rather than a robo-advisor, which is like a glorified online calculator, a fiduciary financial advisor who is also a CFP® will take the time to get to know you personally, understand your priorities and concerns, and do what is in your best interests. In fact, the CFP® designation includes an ethics component. By seeking an advisor who is a CFP®, you can increase the chances that your best interests will be taken care of. Your advisor should provide expert, tailored financial guidance that will help you manage risks and reach your most important financial goals. He or she can take into account specific situations, such as how best to manage a lump-sum inheritance, or help you figure out how best to pay off your mortgage or whether to hold onto or sell a second residence.

4. Understand longevity risk, and manage it as a top concern. Picture what would happen if you outlived your money. How would you cope? What would your life look like if you had no more money? Would you have to deny yourself the basics? Would you go hungry or homeless, or become a burden on family members forced to look after you? These are deeply scary and unpleasant thoughts. Far better to take action now to make sure this doesn't happen. Read on to learn how.

5. Cut back on current expenses to free up money to save for your future. Let's assume that you do your retirement budget and realize that with your current savings, you might not be able to afford the lifestyle that you envision in retirement. You realize that you'll need to save more money, which will mean trimming some expenses. Perhaps you could sell a vacation home, especially if you don't use it that much. You could probably save a lot by moving to a smaller house, which could mean spending less on your mortgage, utilities, property tax, and insurance. If you love to travel, could you choose destinations that are less expensive and closer to home for a few years of turbocharged savings? Think about what you could cut back on in order to save more for your future.

6. Pay yourself first, and keep increasing your retirement contributions. The easy solution is to pay yourself first through automated payroll savings. That way you'll never see the money that goes straight into your retirement account, beginning to accumulate tax-deferred growth without you having to think about it or be tempted to spend the money. If you can save 10 percent of your salary—for example, $7,500 of a $75,000 annual salary—why not increase it by 1 percent of your salary each year? If you do that for five years, you'll be saving close to $4,000 more a year. And that additional savings can keep growing over time.

7. Move to a slightly more aggressive investment mix. You should always stay within your investment risk comfort zone, but some of us are not wisely or appropriately allocated in terms of long-term investments and what matters most. Some very conservative investors fear any risk but don't realize that by avoiding volatility risk and keeping much of their money in a supposedly ultrasafe bank account, money market accounts, certificates of deposit, and government bonds, they might be earning a few percentage points less per year overall compared with someone in a more typical, balanced mix of 60 percent stocks, 30 percent bonds, and 10 percent cash-like conservative investments.

The greatest risks awaiting many retirement investors are the risk of outliving their money (longevity risk) and the risk of not keeping up with inflation and seeing their purchasing power erode over the next few decades. Mainly, though, it's about lost opportunity. Why give up a reasonable potential return of 6 or 7 percent in a moderately aggressive but still diversified mix that you won't need to touch for a few decades just because you prefer less day-to-day volatility?

One way to be able to earn more on your investments is through a well-structured portfolio with distinct tranches or buckets in which you have some short-term investments to cover your shorter-term income needs. These might cover the next one to three years and be more conservative because you can't afford to take much risk of losing your principal investment for short-term goals or needs. You would also have some inter-mediate-term investments to meet goals or needs that extend through the next 10 years. These can involve some more risk and the potential for higher income. Then, having taken care of the next decade, you can afford to have some more-aggressive investments for your longer-term (10 years and longer) needs and goals.

One thing I tell investors who are under the age of 50 is

that the best thing to help their retirement plan is for the stock market to be down for a solid 10 years so that they can accumulate retirement securities at low prices.

8. Delay your retirement and/or your Social Security benefits. If you aren't ready to retire financially or for other reasons, by staying in the workforce for just two more years, you could greatly improve your long-term financial security. Let's imagine that you are close to retirement age but realize that your retirement will be a lot more secure if you keep working a bit longer, let's say for two more years. To see what a difference working two more years could make, start by adding up the additional savings.

Let's say you can save $15,000 for your retirement each year. That's an additional $30,000 in savings. You'll also be funding two fewer years of retirement, which helps reduce the chance of ever running out of money. Additionally, you can push back taking your Social Security benefits by two years, thereby increasing your monthly benefits by 16 percent for the rest of your life.

Let's assume for this illustration that in retirement, you would have to withdraw $40,000 a year from your savings. By working two more years, you'll be adding $30,000 to your retirement savings while needing $80,000 less, for a total net gain of $110,000. That doesn't even include the lifetime net benefit of a 16 percent increase in your monthly Social Security benefits. That gain is tough to estimate, because you'd have to assume how long you'll live, and it would depend on what your annual Social Security benefits would be at your full retirement age, but that could conceivably add up to another $50,000 or

$100,000, depending on a variety of factors.

You can run your own numbers, but just remember that delaying your retirement for a couple of years could be a game changer.

9. Put your retirement ahead of your children's college costs. If you have children, you might be concerned about college costs. If so, be careful *not* to put your children's college funding ahead of your own retirement savings, especially if you have some major catching up to do.

Imagine a scenario in which your kids graduate from university with degrees and little debt. But along the way, you have neglected to save for your own retirement and could be somewhat reliant on them financially in your old age. Instead, wouldn't it be a far better gift to teach them to be financially responsible, financially independent, and select good schools that offer good value (lower tuition), such as an in-state public college, and largely pay their own way?

Meanwhile, you can save diligently for your retirement and spare your kids from any future financial responsibility to take care of you. Rather than try to help them with college now, you'll be acting as a good role model for them in how to manage your money wisely and well. And perhaps down the road, you'll be in a strong enough financial position to be able to help them pay off some of their debt.

Of course, it's great to be able to help your children pay for college. But if you are scrambling to save enough for your own financial security, you have to come first.

10. Consider whether to pay down debt before retiring.
Although some people want to enter retirement mortgage-free, for practical and emotional reasons, it can be desirable to carry a mortgage during your retirement years and continue to pay it off. It can make perfect financial sense to keep paying mortgage at 3 or 4 percent interest rather than be in a rush to pay it down early. That way you can also let retirement account investments continue to grow on a tax-deferred or tax-free basis rather than diverting those higher-yielding investments elsewhere. However, if you can fully pay off your mortgage and any other debt, other than perhaps a nominal low-interest auto loan, without financial strain, you could substantially reduce your expenses in retirement and ease your burden, thereby helping to ensure your long-term financial health.

11. Redefine retirement. We've looked primarily at ways to squeeze more money out of your current expenses so that you can save for your future expenses. There's an additional way to resolve any risks of outliving your money. That's by continuing to earn at least some income after you leave a full-time job so that you withdraw less of your savings.

Some women are in careers that lend themselves to "easing into retirement" by working one or two fewer days per week or reducing their daily hours. This is especially true for doctors and nurses or people who are self-employed. Alternatively, you might want to leave the hectic routine of a full-time job and explore a more part-time vocation, such as a massage therapist, caterer, or part-time tax return preparer. Another option is to apply your skills in a different manner, such as a teacher who retires from classroom teaching but works part time with students one on one as a tutor.

After you retire, earning money in a part-time job—even 10 or 15 hours a week—could seriously change the dynamic of your monthly finances, and it could be socially and mentally stimulating. Remember, after your full retirement age, you can collect your full Social Security benefit and earn as much as you wish. You could even increase your Social Security benefit as you continue to pay into the system!

Think about what you could do to enhance your financial future even as you approach retirement.

CHAPTER 17

Going the Distance

I n this final chapter of the "Life Stages" section of the book, we take a deeper look at how to successfully navigate financially throughout your retirement. In brief: make a smart and smooth transition into retirement, manage your money well during retirement so that it lasts at least as long as you will, and make your estate planning intentions clear.

HOW TO MAKE IT TO THE FINISH LINE

These actions can guide you through a successful retirement, addressing your most important financial needs and concerns.

MAKE A SUCCESSFUL TRANSITION INTO RETIREMENT

Setting yourself up for a successful retirement begins with assessing whether you are financially ready to retire. If not, do all you can to keep working, keep saving for your future, and delay the transition from growing your nest egg to drawing it down. Even if you suffer a setback, such as being laid off or surviving a major illness, try to find a way to earn some income if you still need to in order to fund your retirement goals.

The key is to be as intentional and thoughtful as you can before you retire and in choosing how to retire. For example, phased retirement, taking a part-time job in retirement, or following your passion into a second career are all possibilities.

BE CAREFUL ABOUT WHEN YOU CLAIM SOCIAL SECURITY BENEFITS

Deciding when to retire is enormously important, as is opting for the best time to begin to take Social Security benefits. Generally, the later the better, up to age 70. That's because you'll receive an additional 8 percent on your monthly Social Security benefits for each year that you delay taking them.

Unfortunately, many people choose to take these benefits as early as age 62. They're eager to start receiving money ASAP, but they'll permanently receive less each month because of their impatience. Do you think there's at least a 50 percent chance that you'll live past the age of 77 or 78? That's the so-called "breakeven age," after which you'll have a net benefit from waiting from age 62–66 and receiving the additional monthly benefits. The breakeven age after which you'll benefit from waiting from age 62–70 is 80–81. Most people—especially most women—will be better off in the long run by delaying these benefits.

For women, who generally earn less than men—and therefore tend to save less than men and receive smaller Social

Security benefits based on those smaller earnings—*and* live longer, it's prudent to do everything you can to increase your monthly Social Security benefits. Chances are you'll need those additional benefits, *and* you'll live long enough to truly appreciate them. The average 65-year-old American female can expect to live to age 86.6, according to the Social Security Administration.

However, there are exceptions. For some women, it could make sense to claim your Social Security benefits early if there are health-related concerns and financial constraints.

Poor health: If you are in poor health, you may no longer be able to work. You may also not expect to live as long as the average person. If you're no longer earning a salary, you may need Social Security benefits to get by. In this case, you may be better off claiming Social Security payments now.

Financial constraints: Perhaps you're in a financial bind despite your best efforts. If so, you'll appreciate any source of income as soon as possible. In this case, it might make sense to claim Social Security benefits as soon as you're eligible. However, that scenario doesn't fit with the profile of a typical middle-class millionaire woman, who works diligently to prepare for retirement and who is in a good place financially because of frugal living and diligent saving.

However, if you don't fit into one of those two groups—ill health or financially desperate—you'll likely benefit from waiting as long as you can to begin receiving your Social Security checks.

Another reason to be careful about taking these benefits early is that if you're still working or receiving other income, your Social Security benefits will be reduced by $1 for every

$2 beyond $18,240 in earnings in 2020. That applies if you're below full retirement age for the full year. If you work during the year in which you reach your full retirement age, you can earn up to $48,600 before Social Security benefits are reduced by $1 for every $3 earned.[20]

It's important to understand your full retirement age (FRA) before you decide to receive benefits. It's based on your date of birth—currently age 66 but gradually rising to 67 over the next five years. So, if you were born between 1954 and 1960, your FRA is between 66 and 67. Anyone born in 1960 or later has an FRA of 67—unless Congress modifies these ages at some point.

I think that's a great incentive to wait at least until after you stop working full time before you begin to collect Social Security benefits.

CLAIMING STRATEGIES FOR COUPLES

There have been some important considerations for claiming Social Security that apply to couples. Couples should review their options so that they can get the most from their combined benefits. Factors to consider include both of your ages, your health status, and your respective benefits. A lower-earning spouse could receive a substantial survivor benefit based on a deceased, higher-earning spouse's benefit.

For a couple with similar earnings histories and life expectancy, it might make sense for both spouses to delay their

---

[20]   https://www.ssa.gov/pubs/EN-05-10069.pdf

benefits to age 70. But if there are major differences in work history and earnings, the lower-earning spouse could file earlier, while the higher earner waits until age 70. That way you could get the most out of the higher benefit. In many cases, the husband will have earned more and will die before his wife, leaving the widow with a substantial survivor benefit.

BENEFITS FOR DIVORCED COUPLES

A lot of divorced couples might not realize that you can receive benefits based on your ex-spouse's work record if that provides a higher benefit than what you'd receive based on your own work record. That would have no bearing on what the other ex-spouse would receive for his or her own benefits. It's simply an extension of the spousal benefits entitlement. It's an option if your marriage lasted 10 years or longer, you remain unmarried, you're at least age 62, and you and your ex-spouse are eligible for Social Security retirement or disability benefits.

To learn more about applying for Social Security benefits and about claiming strategies, go to the Social Security website.

Beyond Social Security benefits claiming strategies, there are other important decisions as you enter retirement. These involve how to invest, create a reliable stream of retirement income, manage your health-care costs and risks, and, perhaps most importantly, choose a financial advisor whom you can trust to help you through these and other vital decisions.

IDENTIFY, UNDERSTAND, AND
MANAGE YOUR KEY RISKS

Understand the trade-offs involved in managing risks. Begin by identifying your most relevant or important risks. For retirees, the most important challenge is to make sure you don't run out of money before you die.

People in their 60s and older also need to be aware of inflation risk—not seeing their purchasing power erode—as well as volatility. As you age, you should have less money exposed to the stock market, but a common mistake is to go too far too quickly toward a portfolio that doesn't have enough growth potential. However, some retirees were overexposed to stocks during the 2008 financial crisis. Imagine having 80 percent of your retirement money in stocks and seeing the value of your retirement portfolio slashed almost in half. Some people then panicked and sold stocks near the market bottom, locking in their losses. Others, who had the patience to sit and wait, were rewarded for that patience, but their portfolios didn't fully recover for several years. Being aware of and managing all risks can be a challenge. The next step shows you how.

WORK WITH TRANCHES OR BUCKETS TO
TAKE CARE OF ALL OF YOUR NEEDS

As mentioned briefly in the previous chapter, an effective way to address a broad variety of financial risks is to set up a system of tiers or buckets in your investment portfolio. Think of the short term, medium term, and long term as three separate financial focuses. By addressing all three in separate buckets or tiers, you can create a thorough, cohesive system. The short-term bucket acts as a safety buffer against volatility. The medium-term bucket provides a steady flow of income for years. And the long-term bucket is dedicated to maximum long-term growth.

For your *short-term needs* (the next one to three years), you should put money that you can't afford to lose in stable, conservative investments that will be there for you no matter what. This could include a bank savings account, certificates of deposit, and money market accounts, along with perhaps short-term government bonds that have little risk of losing principle. For example, the Bloomberg Barclays 1–5 Year Government Index lost money in only one calendar year in the last decade, in 2013, when it had a loss of 0.12 percent. In most years, it tended to earn between 1 and 4 percent.[21] The key word: safety.

For your *medium-term concerns* (the next three to five or even ten years), income generation is important. Because your short-term bucket is all about safety, and you won't expect to withdraw from the medium-term bucket for a few years, you can have a modest exposure to risk. That can give you the potential to earn more than your short-term investments, with less volatility than your long-term investments, whose purpose is maximum growth. This medium-tier set of investments could include a mix of bonds (corporate and longer-term government bonds) and/or bond funds. You could also consider some dividend-yielding stocks or stock mutual funds. A balanced mutual fund, with a typical mix of about 60 percent stocks

---

21   https://fundresearch.fidelity.com/mutual-funds/perfor-
      mance-and-risk/315809400

and 40 percent bonds, could provide for both within a single investment. Key word: income.

Now let's look at your *long-term needs*. The most important long-term issue is to make sure you never run out of money. You can address that in part by keeping a large allocation in stocks. Because your first two investment tiers are fairly conservative, dedicated to preserving your money and generating reliable income for the next decade, you can take greater risks in this third tier. That means having more money in stocks and stock mutual funds as well as other volatile and potentially higher-earning assets, such as real estate or commodities. Key word: growth.

This will make it more likely that a portion of your portfolio will be able to grow throughout your life and beyond, in the event that you're able to pass on an inheritance to your loved ones. If you base your time horizon on their lives rather than yours, you can take on even greater risk. That way you can increase your opportunity to earn higher long-term returns, even in your 80s or 90s. This applies to cases where you're confident that you'll have some money to pass on to your heirs.

CONSOLIDATE AND SIMPLIFY YOUR FINANCIAL LIFE

When you retire, it's important to simplify your financial life as much as you can. First, who wants to have to wade through unnecessary paperwork with multiple account statements? There's so much more to life. But also, when you have fewer investment accounts from fewer institutions, it's easier to know what your asset allocation is, making decisions is simplified, and managing your money is easier all around. Because of this, if you haven't already consolidated your financial life, make it a priority once you reach retirement. You'll give yourself the gift of time—more time to play with your grandchildren, travel, play golf, or do anything that you desire.

PROTECT YOURSELF AND YOUR LOVED ONES FROM ELDER ABUSE

Elder abuse is a very real concern, and elderly financial abuse has been called "the crime of the 21st century." According to the National Adult Protective Service Association (NAPSA), one in nine seniors has reported being abused, neglected, or exploited within the past year. The vast majority of abusers are family members and trusted others. Neglect is very common, making up more than half of all reported cases of elder abuse in domestic settings.

Financial abuse can happen in many ways. It can take the form of fake charity solicitations, telemarketing scams, and identity theft. Most victims are in their 80s, and women are more likely than men to be victims. Older women are often seen as easy targets by unscrupulous financial salespeople.

Warning signs of financial elder abuse include:

- Unexpected changes in bank account balances or banking practices

- Unauthorized or unexplained account withdrawals

- Disappearance of funds or valuable possessions

- Unanticipated transfer of assets to a family member or friend

- Sudden changes to a will or other key financial or legal documents

- Allowing a new friend or trusted acquaintance to make decisions on behalf of the elderly person

You can help prevent elder financial abuse by creating a strong support system of people who can keep an eye on elderly family members and loved ones. If you suspect someone is being exploited, take action as soon as you recognize warning signs. Notify the proper authorities. Confront the abuser directly. If you suspect an elderly family member has been abused or defrauded, ask her or him directly. Too often we're afraid to act unless we're certain that abuse is occurring.

Additional actions can include:

- Checking in regularly with an aging relative who lives alone

- Monitoring who visits the elderly person's home

- Asking to cosign their bank account

- Having the elderly person sign a durable power of attorney, appointing someone trustworthy

- Using or having your parents use a fiduciary to handle money

ADDRESS YOUR HEALTH-CARE AND
LONG-TERM CARE NEEDS

Whether you've had employer-sponsored health-care benefits or have been on your own to purchase health insurance during your working years, as you enter retirement, everything will change, beginning with signing up for Medicare coverage. Medicare is complicated, including Parts A, B, and D. (There is no Part C.)

There also are various other options, including Medicare Advantage, an all-in-one plan that combines Parts A, B, and D. There are also supplemental/"Medigap" policies that are offered privately to help with out-of-pocket expenses or to provide coverage when outside of the United States.

Let's keep this fairly high level. The keys to know are:

- Part A pays for hospital costs after a deductible, and most people don't pay a premium for Medicare Part A.

- Part B is optional coverage for medical expenses. This includes doctor visits and medical equipment. You pay an annual premium based on your income. Part B covers 80 percent of "Medicare-approved" costs, and you're responsible for the remaining 20 percent of the cost. You can sign up for Medicare Part B during a seven-month enrollment window that begins three months before the month in which you turn 65, and it ends three months afterward. If you miss this window, you could have a gap in coverage and pay a penalty.

- Part D is optional prescription-drug coverage and involves an additional premium.

Medicare does *not* cover long-term care costs. Roughly one in two people who turn 65 will need some type of long-term care at some point. Because women live longer, they have a greater chance of needing long-term care. Almost two in three women (64 percent) will spend some time in a nursing home, according to a 2017 study by the Rand Corporation.[22]

The cost of long-term care can vary from region to region or city to city, but more importantly, it depends on the type of care you'll need. These are the national average annual costs for several types of care, according to the 2019 Genworth Cost of Care Survey:

- Home health aide: $52,624

- Adult day care: $19,500

- Assisted living facility: $48,612

- Nursing home, private room: $102,200

- Nursing home, semiprivate room: $90,155

The challenge with long-term care is it is a crapshoot as to whether you'll need it and, if you do need it, how long you're going to require care. The average woman will need nursing home care for 301 days, according to the Rand study. A study by the Lincoln Financial Group says that 75 percent of nursing home stays will be 240 days or fewer, with 10 percent lasting 2.75 years and 5 percent having to stay for four years or longer. That four-year stay in a nursing home might set you back

---

[22] https://www.pnas.org/content/114/37/9838

roughly $400,000. But you only face a 5 percent chance of that. Can you afford to take that chance?

That's what insurance is for. You'll need to weigh the cost versus the probability of needing the care. Another option is to "self-insure," which is another way of saying that if you don't buy long-term care insurance, make sure to save substantially and separately in order to have money to pay for these late-life costs if needed. Your financial advisor can help you think this through and help you make the best decision for your situation.

CONSIDER A HEALTH SAVINGS ACCOUNT

There's a special savings account with a lot of flexibility to which you can contribute money on a pretax basis to pay for qualified medical expenses. Health savings accounts (HSAs) actually offer a triple tax advantage: in addition to tax-deductible contributions, money that is in the account can grow tax-free. Then any withdrawals for qualified medical expenses are also tax-free. Finally, once you reach retirement age, you can use the assets for any expense, not just medical expenses.

You need to have a high-deductible health plan to be able to contribute to an HSA. For 2020, the minimum deductible for a high deductible health plan is $1,400 for an individual and $2,800 for a family. And for 2020, you can contribute up to $3,550 for self-only coverage and up to $7,110 for family coverage in an HSA. What's more, HSA funds roll over from one year to the next if you don't spend them.

TAKE GOOD CARE OF YOUR ESTATE

Estate planning is another critical part of financial planning. It's important, of course, to have a will, which should include an executor and up-to-date beneficiaries, and be up to date to reflect any major changes in your life. In addition, there are several other key elements to include:

Living will: This can guide your family clearly on your end-of-life wishes regarding do-not-resuscitate (DNR) and other orders.

Powers of attorney: There are two types of powers of attorney. A medical, or health care, power of attorney gives someone whom you name the authority to make decisions on your behalf regarding your health care if you are no longer able to. Similarly, a durable, or financial, power of attorney can give a person or organization that you name the power to act on your behalf regarding financial or business transactions if you're no longer able to.

Trusts are another important tool that you can use to tailor your estate plan and create the most tax-efficient transfer of wealth if appropriate to your circumstances.

A good estate-planning attorney is critically important, and this person can work in coordination with your fiduciary financial advisor to make sure your late-in-life wishes and interests are well taken care of. Finally, it's vitally important that with all these pieces of your estate plan taken care of, you share with your loved ones where all of your financial documents are so that when the time comes, the transition of your estate can happen with as little confusion or stress as possible.

SECTION V

Taking Charge

CHAPTER 18
Action Steps to Secure Your Future Today

This book describes the obstacles to financial security faced by millions of women. In summary: As a woman, chances are you'll live longer than the average man but earn less money over your lifetime. As a result, saving enough money could be a challenge, as could making it last.

Making matters worse, there's a good chance that you tend to put the needs of others before your own. While it's wonderful to be caring and compassionate, you also have to take care of your own financial needs. After all, if you don't, who will?

Here are 10 action steps that you can take right now, this week, this month, this year, and beyond. You don't need to do them all at once, but they are important, specific, tangible steps that can make a difference to your financial future.

1. Work with a fiduciary financial advisor. Because we have busy lives and aren't all financial experts, it can be hard to know all that we need to, and it can be a challenge to avoid making financial mistakes. That's why it can help to work with a professional advisor, someone who, by design and legal obligation, puts your interests first and foremost in everything he or she does.

2. Take charge. In addition to working with a professional, who can guide you well, learn more about finances. You needn't be an expert, but know enough to be confident and comfortable thinking about your finances, making financial decisions, or at least discussing your options with a base of knowledge and comfort. By being more involved in your financial affairs, you'll increase the chances of success, however you define that. Most importantly, you'll no longer be vulnerable in the case of an unforeseen setback, such as the death of your spouse or a divorce.

3. Plan. When it comes to personal finances, too many people don't have a plan. They just go paycheck to paycheck or take a haphazard approach to saving, spending, and investing. Without a plan, how do you reach your goals? So make a plan. Think about your financial priorities. Set goals. What do you want or need to save for? How will you invest that money, and over what time period? Whether your long-term goals include a comfortable retirement, a special vacation, a new car, college for the kids, or a paid-off mortgage, make a plan in order to achieve those goals.

4. Advocate. Put yourself first, and advocate for yourself. That's easier said than done, some people will say. True. That's why it should be a priority action step. So what does this look like?

For one thing, when you are about to say yes to some other

demand on your time or resources, take a step back and think about the request, and consider what you might be giving up in order to fulfill this request for someone else. I'm not saying you should suddenly be selfish, but don't just automatically say yes to everything for others if you're short-changing yourself. Think it through and question whether it is too big a sacrifice. In short, it's okay to say no sometimes.

Putting yourself first should mean more than just saying no to others. Say yes to yourself. In one case, a married woman who was our client was affected by pressure from her husband. She had the financial resources to do her own thing, including taking a dream vacation in Europe, but she denied herself this until after the divorce, when she finally said, "I deserve this!" She took the vacation and she loved it.

Can you advocate for yourself? Think about what that means in practical terms, and try it out. You might like it.

5. Budget. Budgeting isn't rocket science. It involves tracking expenses and making sure you don't overspend; allocating money for priorities, such as saving for something specific; and limiting your spending to what you can afford without incurring too much debt. It involves making conscious and disciplined choices. It might not be fun or easy, but it's the cornerstone of building wealth, which happens over time when you consistently spend less than you earn.

6. Save. Once you are following a budget and regularly saving money, you can turn the dial higher and intentionally save more money. That might involve making some thoughtful choices and perhaps some tough ones. Maybe you dine out less, go on a more modest vacation, or drive your car longer. Life is full of trade-offs unless you're ultrawealthy. See how you can save more money. Your future self will thank you. How can you do this? Look at your budget and make conscious choices, and then make it happen.

7. Invest. You have to be true to yourself, your risk tolerance, your time line, your goals and priorities, and your personality as an investor. Remember what we discussed in Chapter 4 about only investing money that's over and above your cash reserve "buffer" or that is earmarked for long-term goals that are at least 10 years away, such as retirement or college expenses. When you understand why you're investing and that markets go through ups and downs, you'll be able to tolerate more risk. However, if you're simply wired to be on the conservative side when it comes to investing, you'll simply need to save more money or wait longer to reach your long-term financial goals.

Higher risk tends to go hand in hand with higher long-term potential investment returns because taking risks tends to get rewarded. Low-risk investments, such as money market investments and certificates of deposit, have low returns. When you use the right investments for the right goals, you'll be able to weather storms and enjoy opportunities during your life's journey.

8. Manage risk. I just referred to low-risk investments. What I could have said or written was "low-volatility" investments. Volatility is what we usually mean when we refer to risk. It's the up-and-down movement of prices in stocks, bonds, and other investments. But there are other enormously important and relevant risks to manage. These include:

- Longevity risk: the risk of running out of money.

- Inflation risk: the risk that your investment returns will be lower than the rate of inflation, which would cause your purchasing power to decline. In other words, your money would buy less in the future.

- Credit risk: the risk that a company that issues a bond that you invest in will default on its debt to you and you won't get all your money back.

- Liquidity risk: the risk that you won't be able to sell an investment quickly when you want to.

- Concentration risk: the risk that your investments are overly concentrated in a single company, industry, sector, region, or type of asset, such as stocks.

Think about these risks and about which ones you're exposed to. Then consider how you can manage those risk exposures effectively.

9. Make it happen. Set goals. Measure your progress. Celebrate your success. You are in charge. Having read this book, you should "get it." You should realize why you need to step up your game financially, and you should understand how to do it. Now make it happen.

10. Be a role model. Did you have a role model growing up who acted in such a way that you just needed to follow their actions and you'd be fine? If that's true, you have a major advantage over someone who didn't have that role model. Now you can be that role model that you might have had or wished you had. Make the right choices for you, but realize that others—perhaps your children, nieces and nephews, or grandchildren—are watching and will likely be shaped by your actions.

I completed this book as the 2020 coronavirus pandemic created turmoil in global financial markets and sent the economy into its deepest plunge since the Great Depression. The economic impact of the pandemic has greatly affected the financial markets and women's current and future financial plans.

A key takeaway is that life is a roller coaster, with plenty of surprising ups and downs. You'll inevitably experience highs and lows in your personal life and career. They might take the form of an individual setback, such as a divorce or a sudden job loss. Or you could be affected by something much larger, such as the bursting of the tech bubble and the ensuing bear market in 2000, the 2008 financial crisis, or the COVID-19 financial fallout.

Whether you are faced with something micro (small scale) or macro (more global in nature), being prepared and understanding your options will give you the confidence to navigate through your challenges. I hope that by reading this book, you will feel equipped with the knowledge and motivation to take steps today to strengthen your financial situation. Remember, you are not alone. We have many clients who wanted to share their experiences in order to help other women. I admire the sense of community women have to support one another through life's curveballs.

There you have it: a road map for how to be a successful middle-class millionaire woman. You can do it! As stated in *Middle-Class Millionaire: Surprisingly Simple Strategies to Grow and Enjoy Your Wealth*, the middle-class millionaire sees personal finance as a lifelong process. The fact that someone has $1 million or more in net worth or in investable assets is just a detail. Money does not define middle-class millionaire women. It's simply a tool they can use to enhance their lives and achieve financial security.

Middle-class millionaire women may differ in a variety of ways, but what they all have in common is they know that success is not a destination. Success is the middle-class millionaire's journey.

I hope this book teaches you some valuable lessons that you can apply to your personal finances no matter where you are on your journey, and I hope it inspires you toward success.

Enjoy the journey.

GLOSSARY

Annuities/Annuitize: An *annuity* is a financial product in which the annuitant (the person buying the annuity) purchases a stream of guaranteed income, typically for life. One way to provide some form of guaranteed income for life is to *annuitize* some assets so as to make sure you'll have a stream of income, in addition to Social Security benefits, throughout your life. Annuities can be fixed or variable, deferred or immediate.

Asset allocation: The act of creating a mix of portfolio assets that reflects your individual time line and risk tolerance, among other factors.

College savings accounts—529 college plans, custodial accounts: College savings accounts can take a number of forms. The two most popular are 529 state college savings plans and custodial accounts—Uniform Gifts to Minors Act (UGMA) and Uniform Transfers to Minors Act (UTMA).

Concentration risk: Concentration risk comes from having too much money invested in a single stock or other investment or in a group of investments that are in the same industry or economic sector. The risk comes from the chance that all the investments would lose value together if something happened to that one company, industry, or sector. Diversification can lower this risk.

Credit ratings: The evaluation of the credit risk of a prospective debtor. The issuers of bonds, such as companies and governments, are rated according to their assessed level of riskiness based on their credit rating. Similarly, people are rated based on certain criteria and are judged for their creditworthiness when applying for loans, mortgages, or even rental leases.

Dividends: The regular payment of a designated share of profits by a company to its shareholders on a per-share basis.

Dollar-cost averaging: The practice of investing the same dollar amount at regular time intervals, such as once a month. By buying the same dollar value, you purchase more shares when the price falls and fewer shares when it rises.

Fiduciary: A person who acts on behalf of another person or persons to manage assets. A fiduciary has a legal and ethical responsibility to act in good faith and trust.

Health savings accounts (HSAs): A savings account dedicated to paying for medical costs. HSAs are tax deductible, and earnings are tax-free. In addition, withdrawals for qualified expenses are tax-free.

Home equity line of credit: When you build equity in your home, you can use that equity to obtain low-cost funds in the form of a "second mortgage"—either a home equity loan or a home equity line of credit (HELOC). HELOCs are a revolving source of funds, much like a credit card, that you use as you see fit.

Individual retirement account (IRA): Investment account intended for retirement savings. It allows earnings to accumulate on either a tax-deferred basis (traditional IRAs) or a tax-free basis (Roth IRAs). The key difference between a traditional IRA and Roth IRA is that with a traditional IRA, you receive a tax break up front through a tax-deductible contribution, but you pay taxes on withdrawals; with a Roth IRA, you don't receive a tax break until you withdraw from the account. At that time, as long as certain conditions are met, you pay no taxes on the amount contributed to the Roth IRA or any earnings.

Leverage: The use of borrowing money when investing. Leverage can magnify your potential investment losses as well as your potential gains.

Liquidity: The ability to easily turn assets or investments into cash. At one extreme, things like real estate have poor liquidity, while money in the bank has high liquidity. Short-term savings should have high liquidity, because you might need to access them at any time.

Living will: A written statement detailing your desires regarding your medical treatment in the event that you are no longer able to express your informed consent. A living will is a type of advance directive.

Longevity risk: The risk of outliving your money.

Medicare: A single-payer national health insurance program that covers seniors and is composed of various parts, including hospital insurance and medical insurance, and prescription-drug coverage.

Money market funds: Mutual funds invested in short-term debt securities, such as U.S. Treasury bills and commercial paper. Money market funds are conservative, short-term investments.

Opportunity cost: The value of what you give up whenever you make a decision. It is the loss of potential gain had you chosen the alternative. If you spend $50,000 on a car, for example, an opportunity cost might be what that money would earn if you invested it instead.

Power of attorney: Written authorization for someone to act on behalf of another person in financial, medical, or other legal matters.

Price-to-earnings ratio, price-to-book ratio, price-to-sales ratio: Forms of stock valuations that use multiples or ratios that divide the stock's estimated value by a metric such as earnings, book value, or annual sales.

Realized and unrealized gains: A realized gain is the gain that is recognized when you sell assets for a price higher than the original purchase price. Until you sell the asset, you have an unrealized, or paper, gain. Selling it realizes the gain. The gain would be taxable if it is not held in a tax-qualified or tax-deferred account, such as an IRA, Roth IRA, or 401(k) plan. You can offset realized gains to reduce the tax implications by selling other assets at a loss.

Realized and unrealized losses: A realized loss is the loss that is recognized when you sell assets for a price lower than the original purchase price. Until you sell the asset, you have an unrealized, or paper, loss. Selling it realizes the loss.

Socially responsible investing (SRI), or social investment: Any investment strategy that considers both financial return and social/environmental good to bring about social change regarded as positive. It is also known as sustainable, socially conscious, "green," or ethical investing. For example, a socially responsible fund might avoid industries that negatively affect the environment and its people. However, it might include companies that produce or invest in alcohol, tobacco, gambling, and weapons. In other words, each investment fund or management team defines how it views social responsibility and why it considers that company socially responsible. Socially responsible investing can mean different things to different people, so it's important to understand the underlying variables and philosophy of the investment and why the investment would be profitable.

Tax-deferred accounts: Accounts (typically retirement accounts) in which investment earnings, including interest, dividends, and capital gains, accumulate tax-free until the investor takes distributions.

Tranche: A portion of something. In a financial context, tranches are separated into short term, medium term, and long term. Each tranche or portion of your portfolio—short-term, medium-term, and long-term—should have a specific purpose and use a dedicated and appropriate set of investments.

Volatility: The tendency for investments, such as the stock market, to rise or fall. More volatile investments often have a higher potential return, while less volatile investments tend to have lower returns. In a sense, investors are rewarded or compensated for accepting volatile investments.

ACKNOWLEDGMENTS

I've wanted to write *Middle-Class Millionaire Women* for a long time to be able to point out the additional hurdles and challenges that women have to overcome versus men. I am grateful and excited that this vision has come to life and want to thank everyone who has helped me get here.

Thank you to my colleague, Carol Petrov, for her valuable input—not only for her insights within this book, but also for sharing her wisdom of financial planning with our clients at Kendall Capital. I also must give a huge shout out to Allan Kunigis. Once again, this book would not be possible without your collaboration, research, writing expertise, and mostly your patience.

Thank you to my wife, Diane, and my three daughters, Whitney, Kelly, and Megan, for your input and enthusiasm for the book.

And last but not least, thank you to my mother, Camille Kendall, who taught me to have passion for helping others. As my mother would say, nobody cares how much you know until they know how much you care. Mom, thank you for your unconditional love, tireless support, and never-ending encouragement.